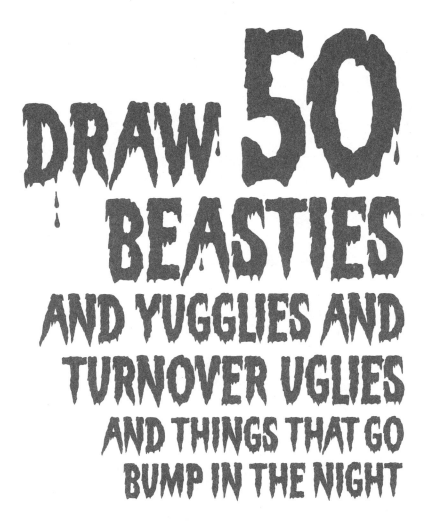

DRAW 50 BEASTIES

AND YUGGLIES AND TURNOVER UGLIES

AND THINGS THAT GO BUMP IN THE NIGHT

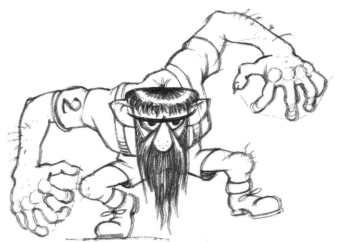

BOOKS IN THIS SERIES

DRAW 50 BEASTIES

AND YUGGLIES AND TURNOVER UGLIES AND THINGS THAT GO BUMP IN THE NIGHT

LEE J. AMES

BROADWAY BOOKS
New York

BROADWAY

Published by Broadway Books
a division of Random House, Inc.
1540 Broadway, New York, New York 10036

BROADWAY BOOKS and it's logo, a letter B bisected on the diagonal, are
trademarks of Broadway Books, a division of Random House, Inc.

Library of Congress Cataloging-in-Publication Data

Ames, Lee J.
    Draw 50 beasties and yugglies and turnover uglies and things that
go bump in the night/Lee J. Ames.—1st ed.
        p.   cm.
    Summary: Provides step-by-step instructions for drawing monsters,
goons, and gruesome beasts.
    1. Drawing—Technique—Juvenile literature.   2. Monsters in art—
Juvenile literature.   [1. Drawing—Technique.   2. Monsters in
art.]   I. Title.   II. Title: Draw fifty beasties and yugglies and
turnover uglies and things that go bump in the night.
NC825.M6A46   1988
743'.6—dc19   88.16143
                    CIP
                    AC

ISBN 0-385-24625-0
      0-385-24626-9 (lib. bdg.)
      0-385-26767-3 (paperback)
Copyright © 1988 by Lee J. Ames and Murray D. Zak

For my grandkids, Lauren, Hilary, and Mark.
For Murray and Moo's grandkids, Melanie and Gregory.
For Warren and Chris's kids, Bryan and Drew.

TO THE READER

Perhaps by now you have come across one of my "Draw 50" books, or perhaps this is the first one you've ever picked up. Either way, I hope to show you in this book how to draw a wide variety of creatures—some creepy, some slimy, and others just plain funny (I hope). Where did I come up with this idea, you may ask? Well, mostly from your suggestions. When I'm not working in my studio, I often travel around the country visiting schools and book fairs, talking to people like you to find out what subjects they like to draw best. I have learned that monsters and strange-looking characters are definitely a favorite.

At first glance, the drawings in this book may appear difficult. But if you take your time and carefully follow the step-by-step instructions for each illustration, you will be able to produce a satisfying finished drawing.

To begin, you will need only clean paper, a pencil with moderately soft lead (HB or No. 2), and a kneaded eraser (available at art supply stores). Select the illustration you want to draw, and then *very lightly and carefully,* sketch out step number one. Then, also very *lightly and carefully,* add step number two to step number one. These steps, which may look the easiest, are the most important. A mistake here can ruin your entire drawing at the end. And remember to watch not only the lines themselves, but the *spaces between the lines* to make sure that they are the same as for the drawing in the book. As you sketch out these first steps, it might be a good idea to hold your work up to a mirror. Sometimes the mirror shows that you've twisted the drawing off to one side without being aware of it.

In each drawing, the new step is shown darker than the previous one so that it can be clearly seen. But you should keep your own work very light. Here's where the kneaded eraser will come in handy; use it to lighten your work after each step.

When you have finished your picture, you may want to go over it with some India ink. Apply this with a fine brush or pen. When the ink has thoroughly dried, erase the entire drawing with the kneaded eraser. The erasing will not affect the India ink.

The most important thing to remember is that even if your first attempts are not as good as you would like them to be, you should not get discouraged. Like any other talent, whether it be performing gymnastic feats or playing the piano, drawing takes practice to do your best.

Though there are many ways to learn how to draw, the step-by-step method used in this book should start you off in the right direction.

TO THE PARENT
OR TEACHER

"Leslie can draw the best beastie I ever saw!" Such peer acclaim and encouragement generate incentive. Contemporary methods of art instruction (freedom of expression, experimentation, self-evaluation of competence and growth) provide a vigorous, fresh-air approach for which we must all be grateful.

New ideas need not, however, totally exclude the old. One such is the "follow me, step-by-step" approach. In my young learning days this method was so common, and frequently so exclusive, that the student became nothing more than a pantographic extension of the teacher. In those days it was excessively overworked.

This does not mean that the young hand is never to be guided. Rather, specific guiding is fundamental. Step-by-step guiding that produces satisfactory results is valuable even when the means of accomplishment are not fully understood by the student.

The novice with a musical instrument is frequently taught to play simple melodies as quickly as possible, well before he or she learns the most elemental scratchings at the surface of music theory. The resultant self-satisfaction, pride in accomplishment, can provide significant motivation. And all from mimicking an instructor's "Do-as-I-do..."

Mimicry is prerequisite for developing creativity. We learn the use of our tools by mimicry. Then we can use those tools for creativity. To this end I would offer the budding artist the opportunity to memorize or mimic (rote-like, if you wish) the making of "pictures"—"pictures" he has been anxious to be able to draw.

The use of this book should be available to anyone who *wants* to try another way of flapping his wings. Perhaps he or she will then get off the ground when a friend says, "Leslie can draw the best beastie I ever saw!"

LEE J. AMES

DRAW 50 BEASTIES

AND YUGGLIES AND TURNOVER UGLIES

AND THINGS THAT GO BUMP IN THE NIGHT

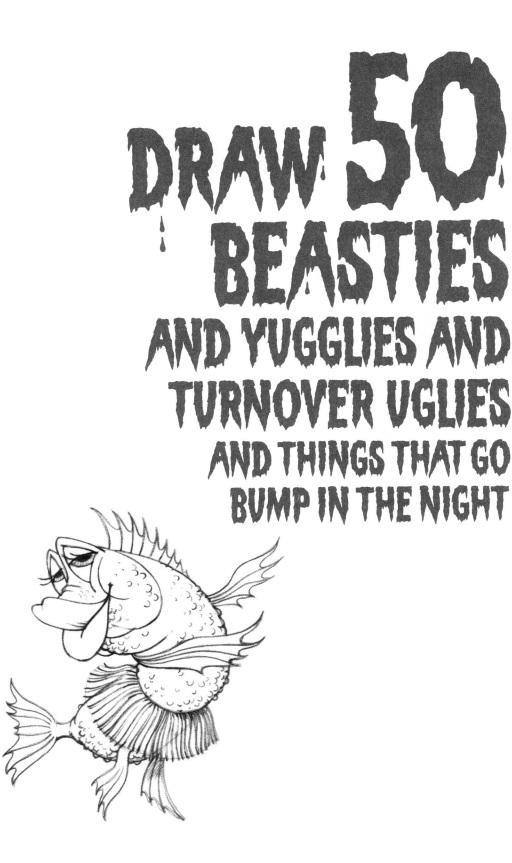

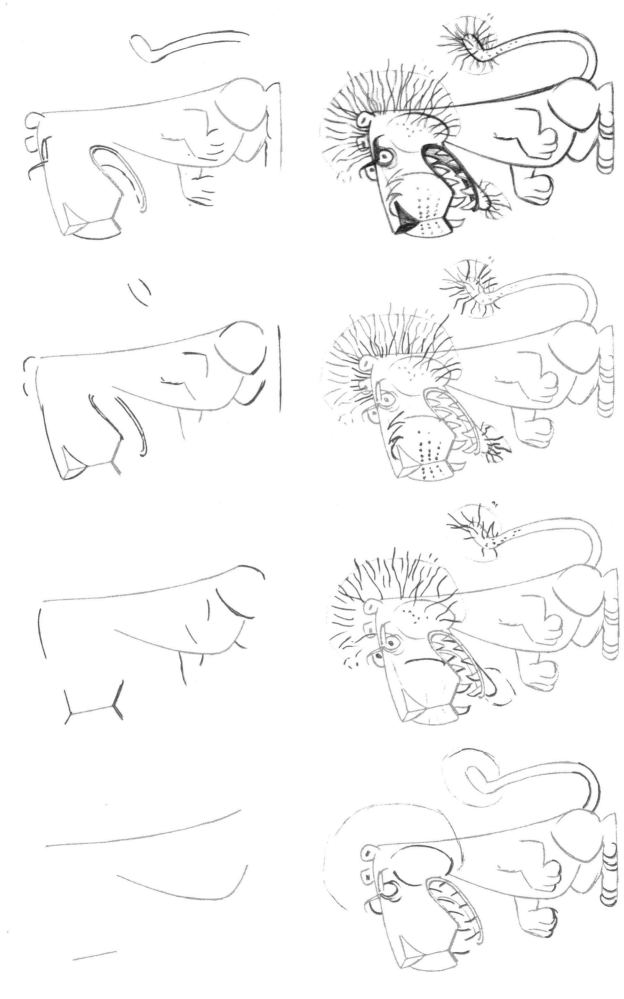

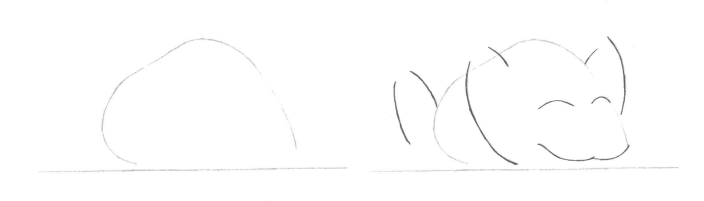

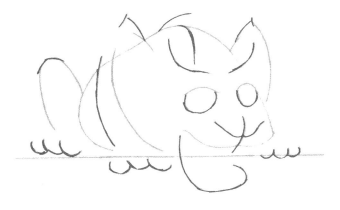
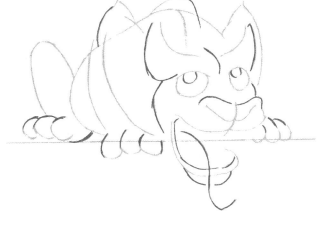

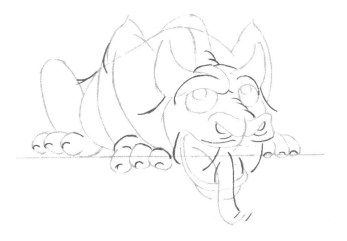
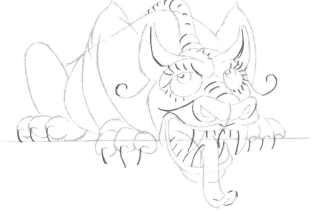

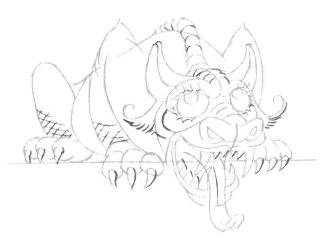
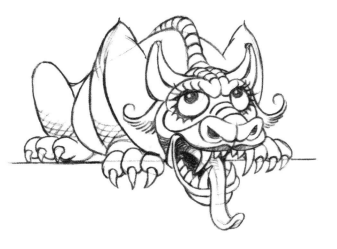

GAR GOYLE

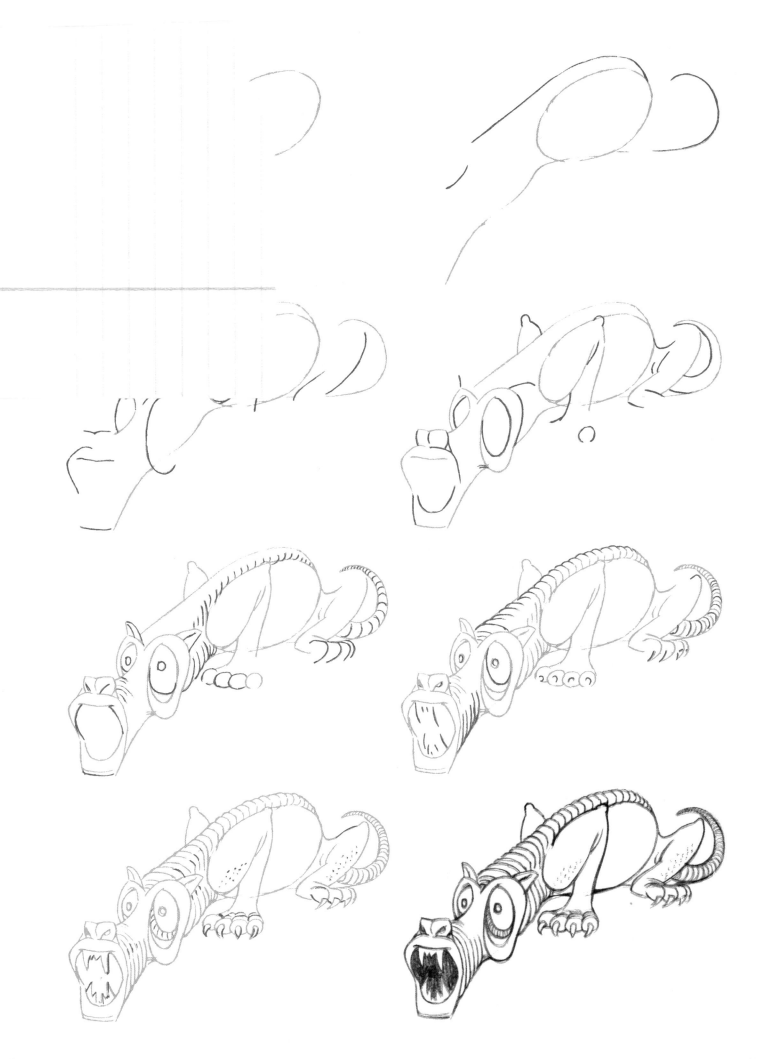

GAR BOY

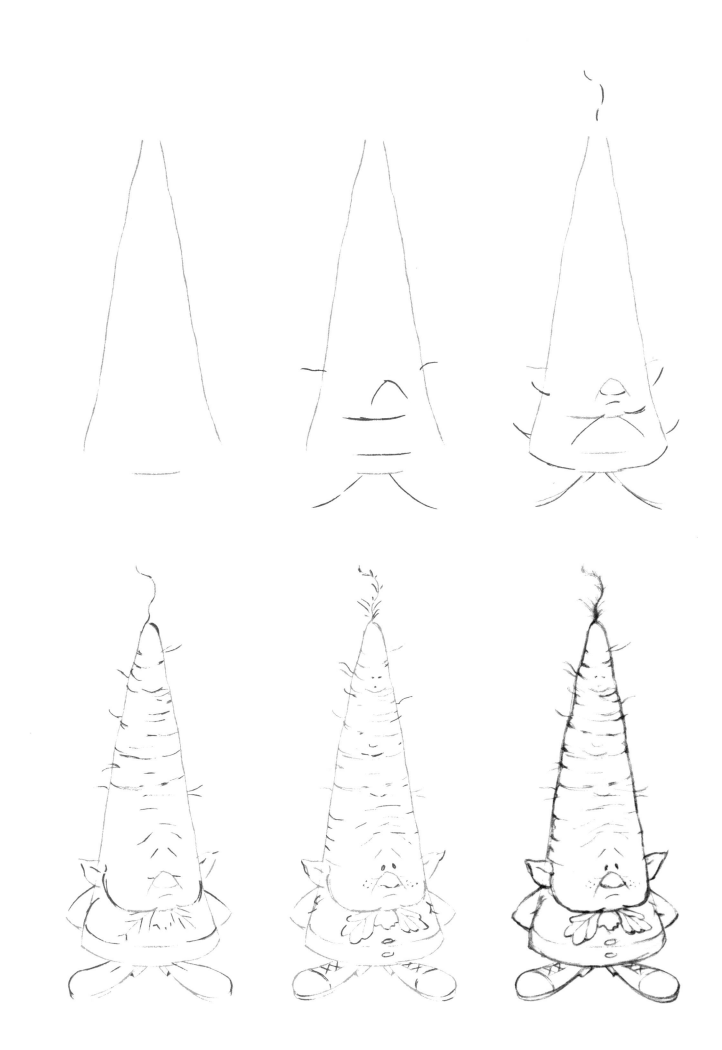

REGGIE VEGEHEAD

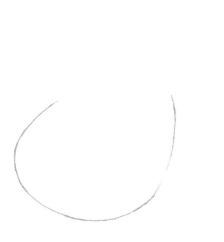
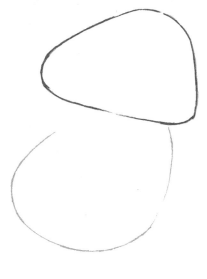
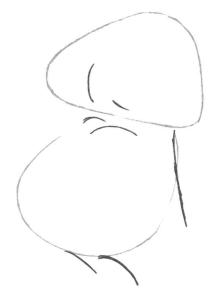
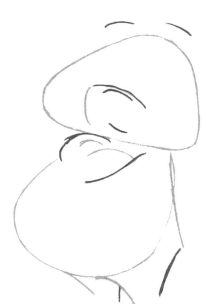
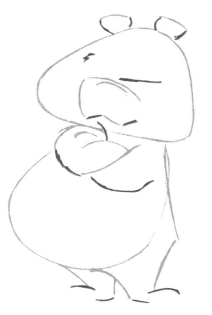
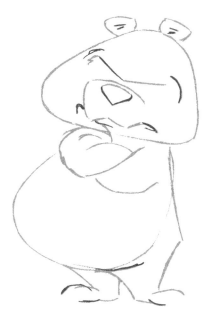
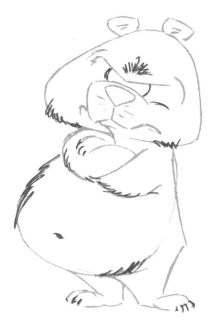
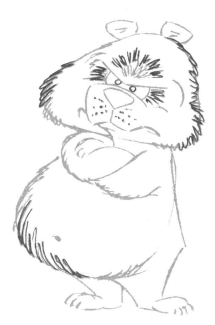
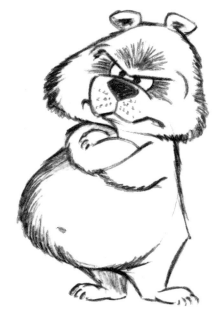

BULLY BELLY BRUNO

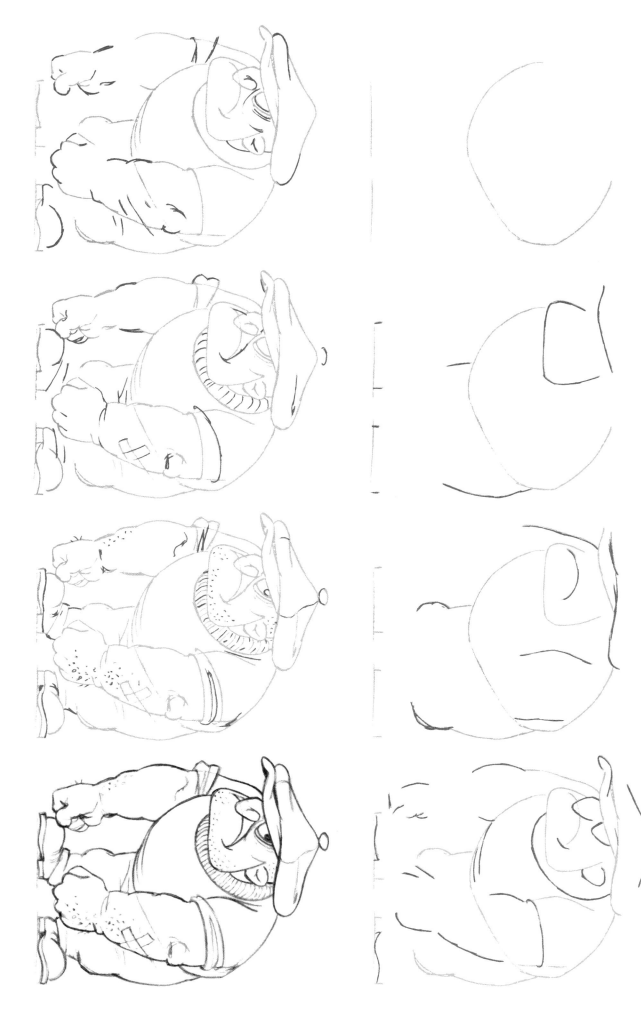

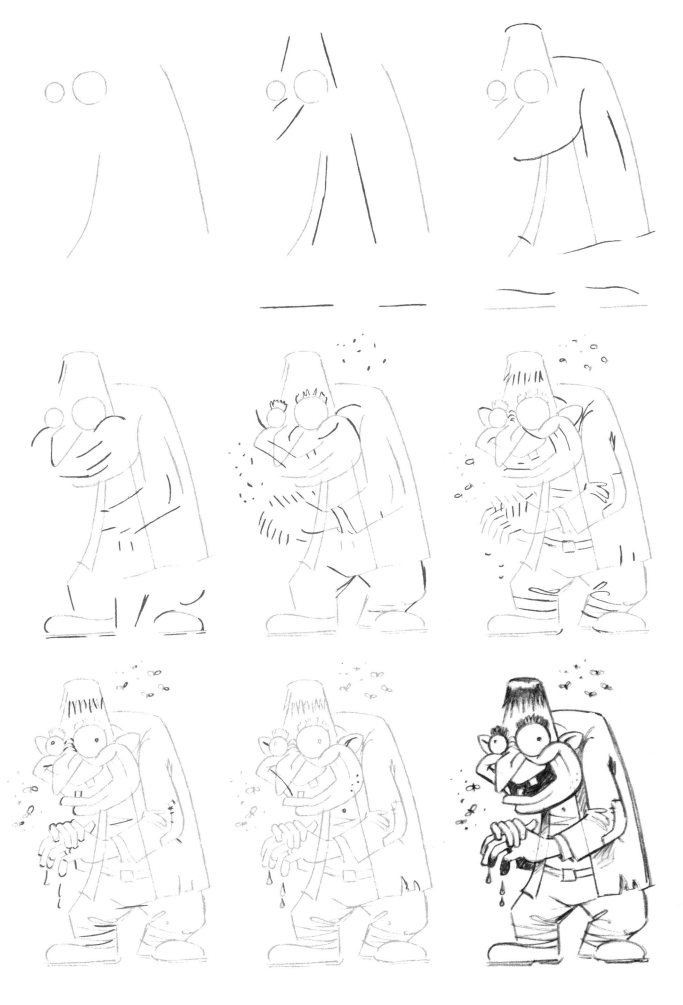

EYE GORE

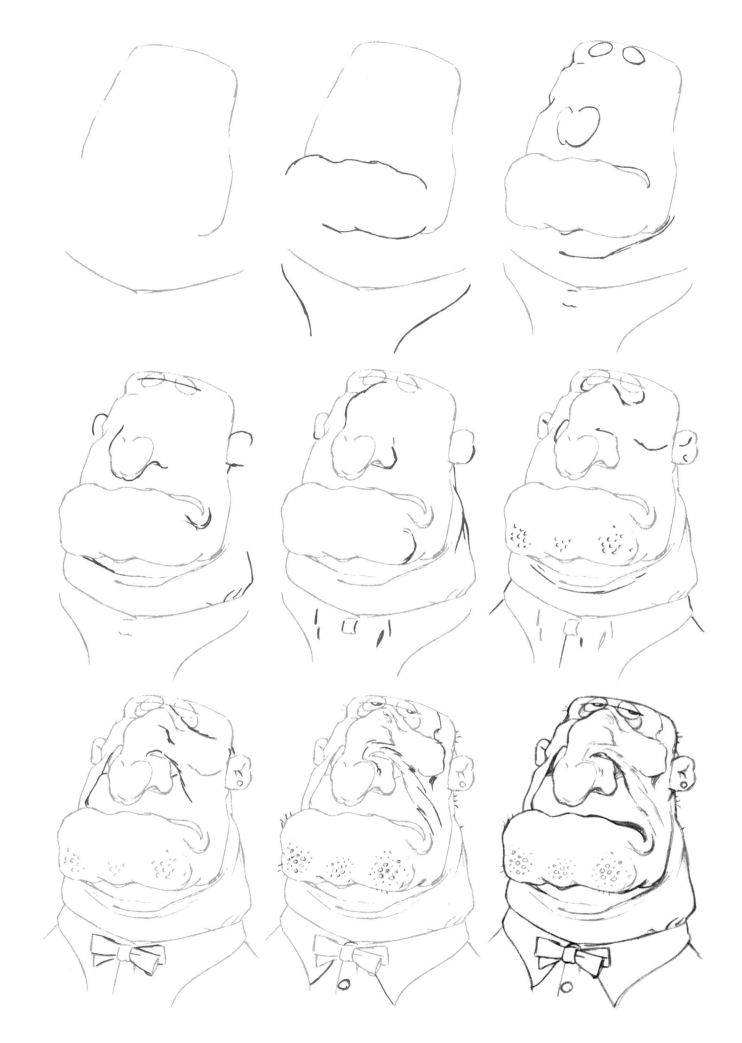

REED DICK YEWLISS

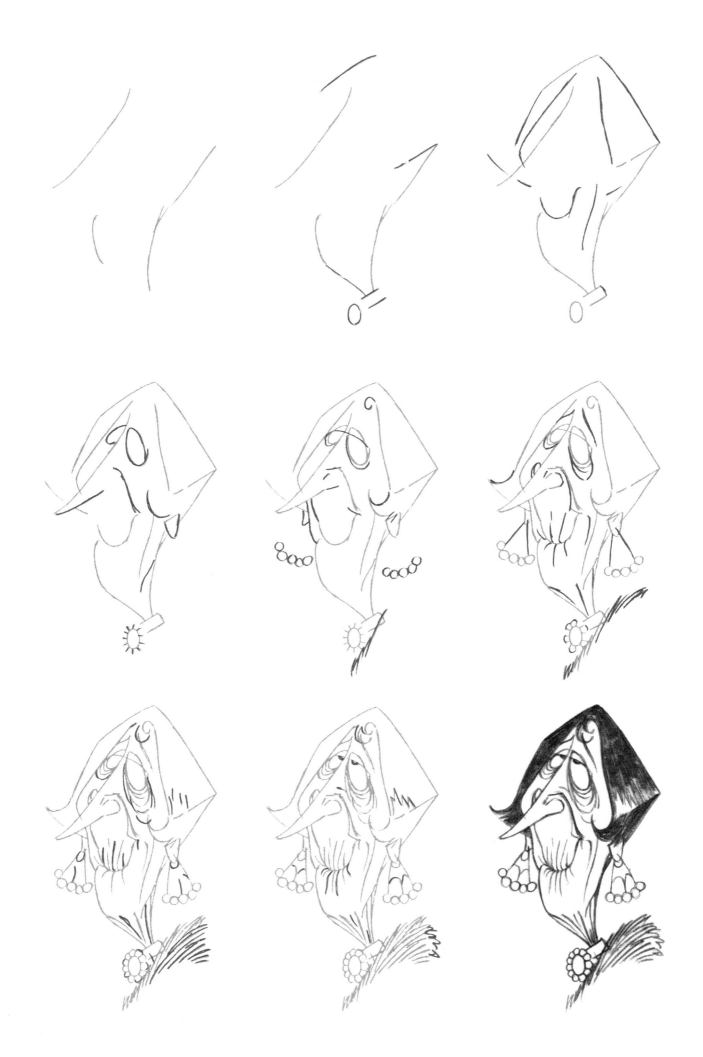

BEA ZARRE

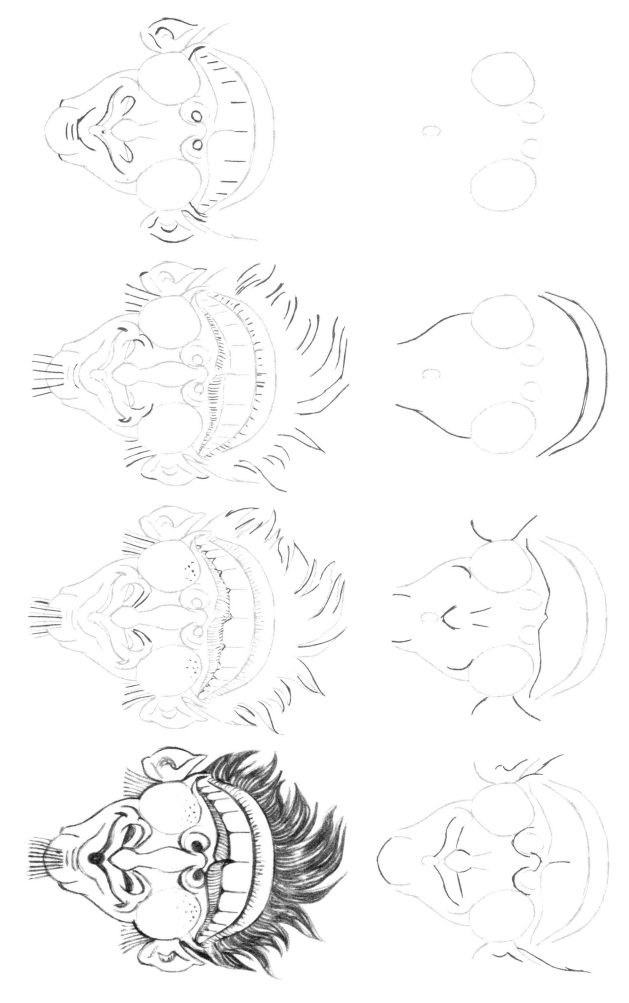

LLEWELLEN NELL EWELL

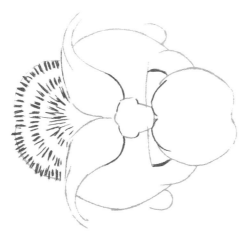

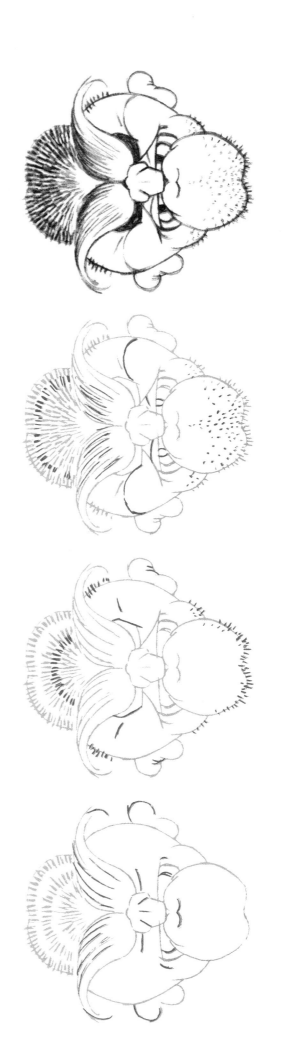

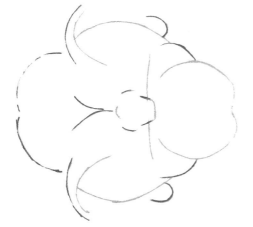

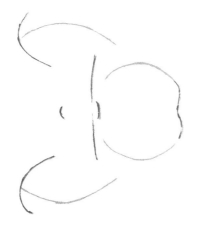

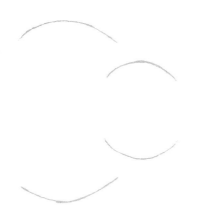

FRANK KNARF

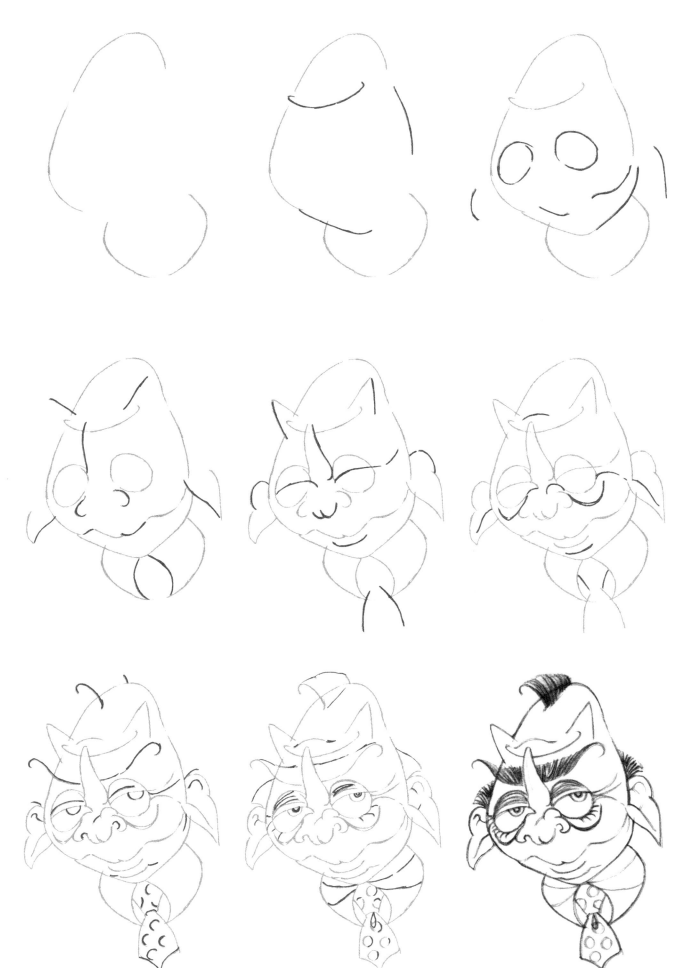

ELBURT TRUBLE

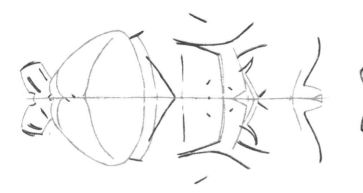
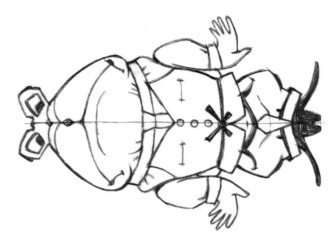
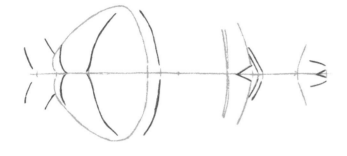
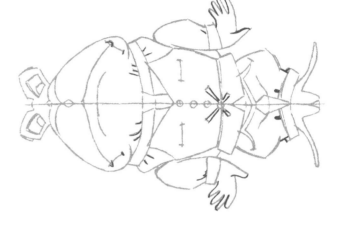
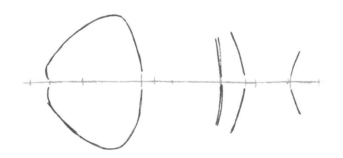
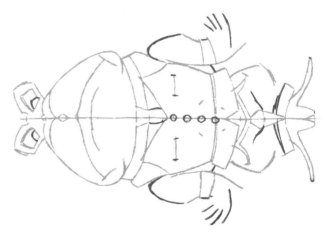
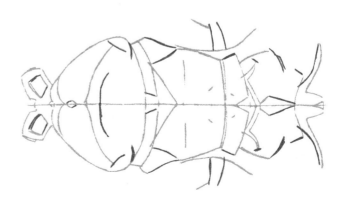

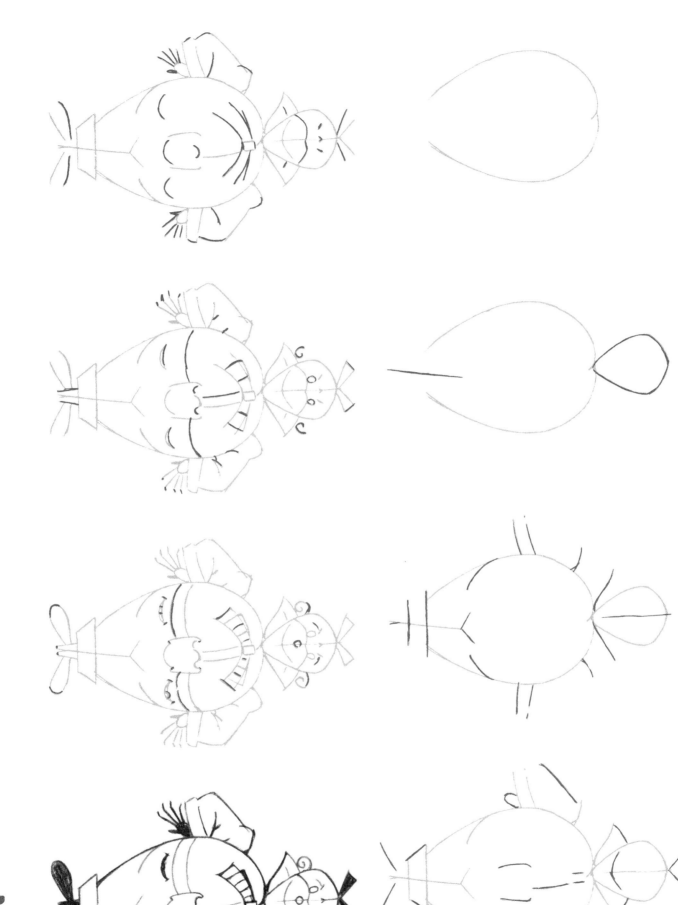

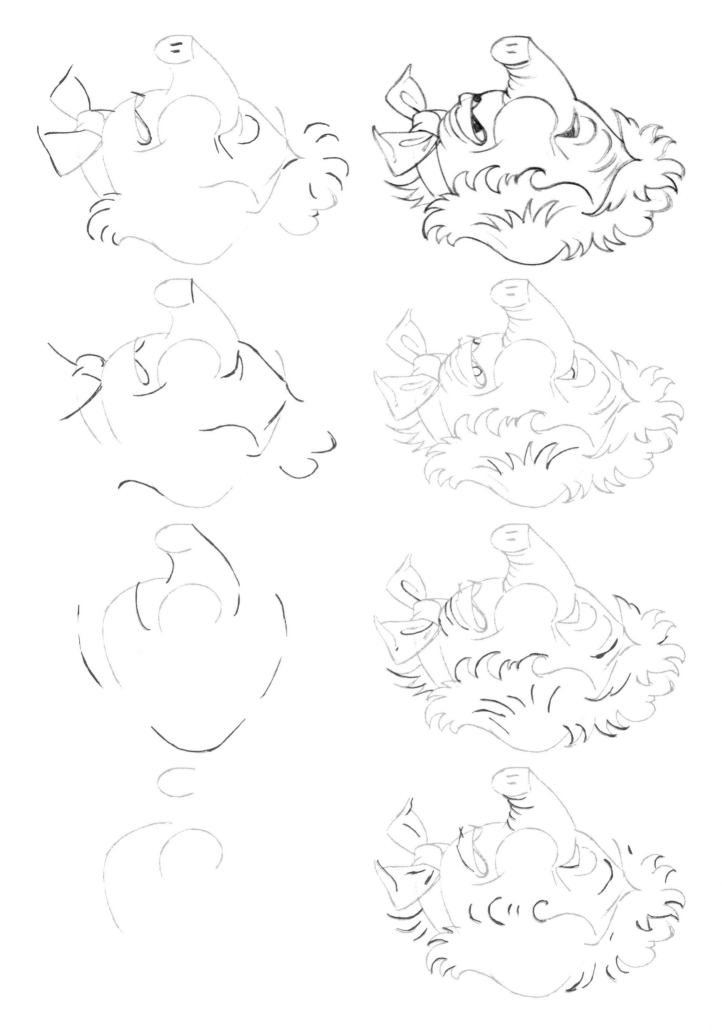

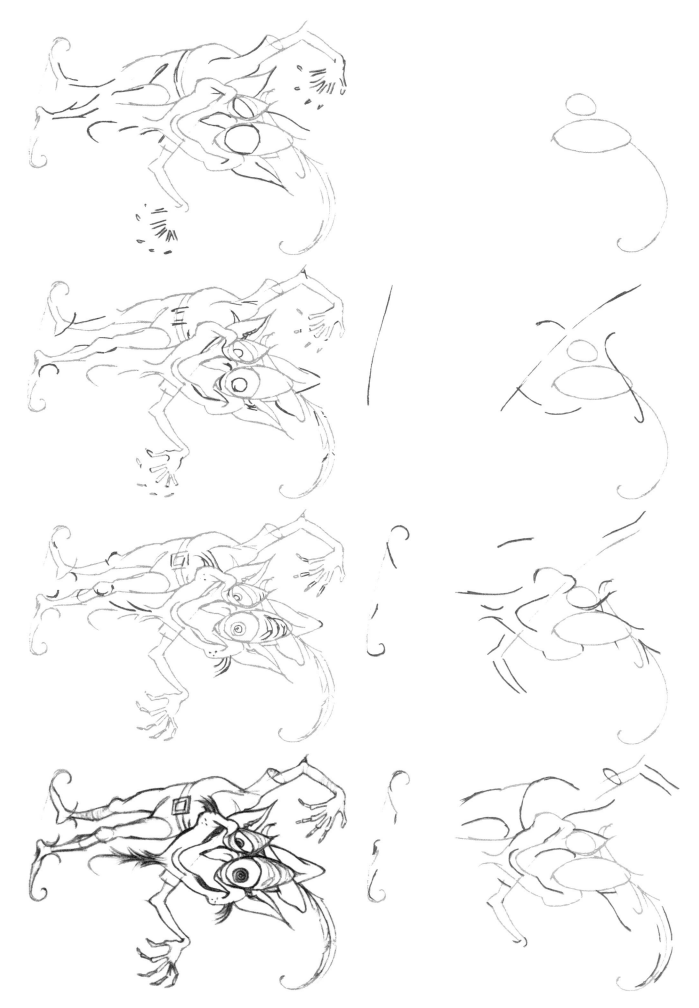

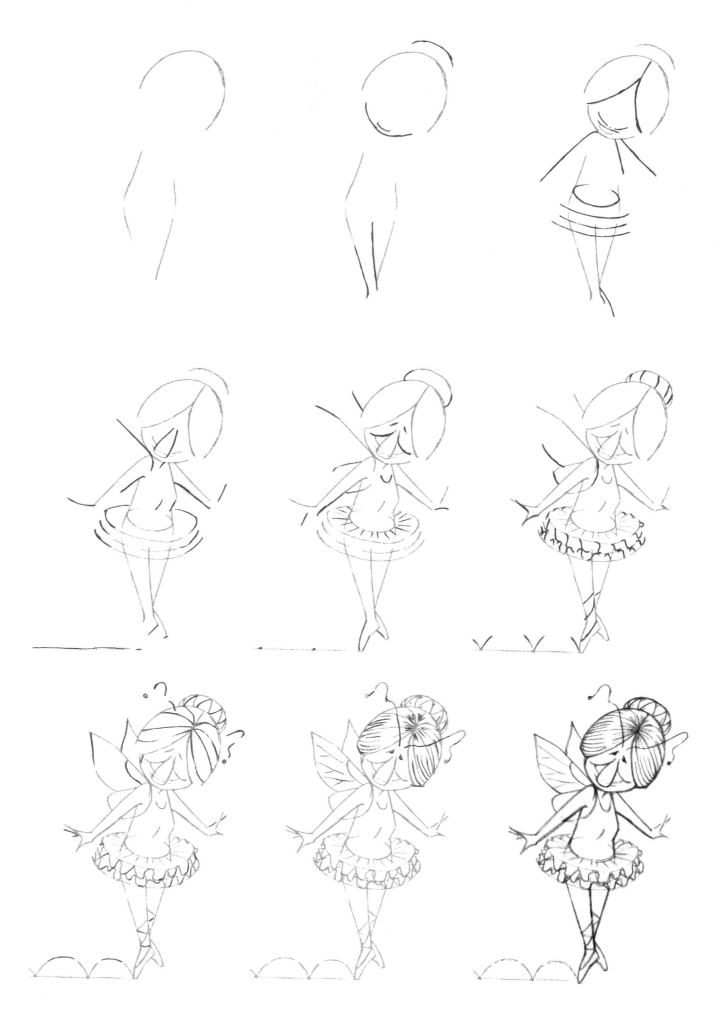

HERZZ ELF

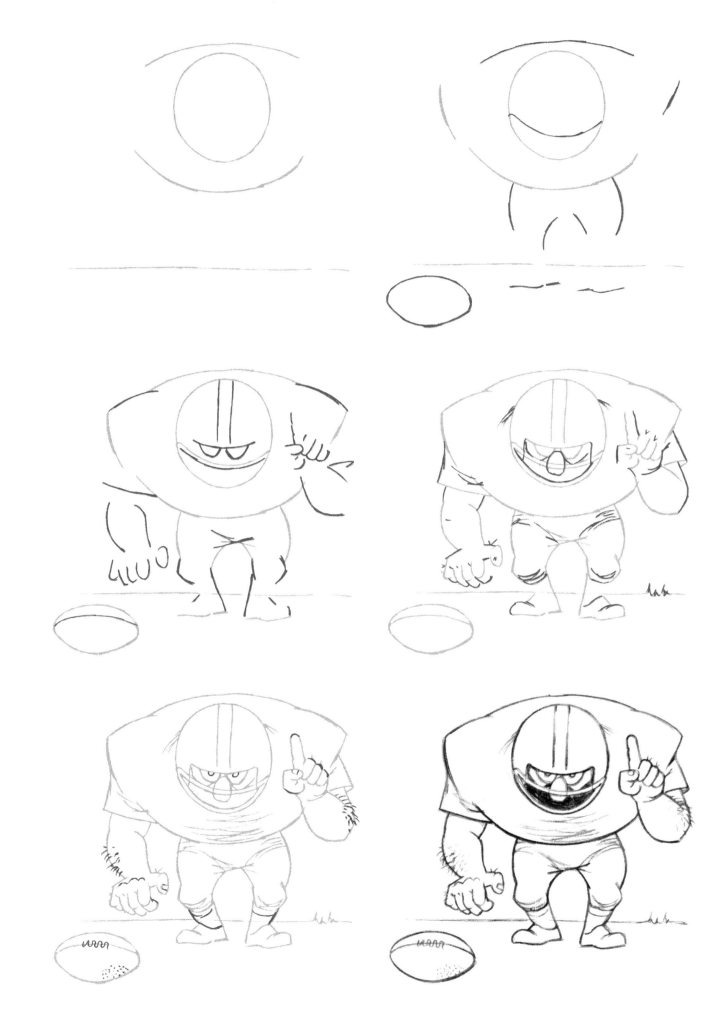

GNOME BURWUN

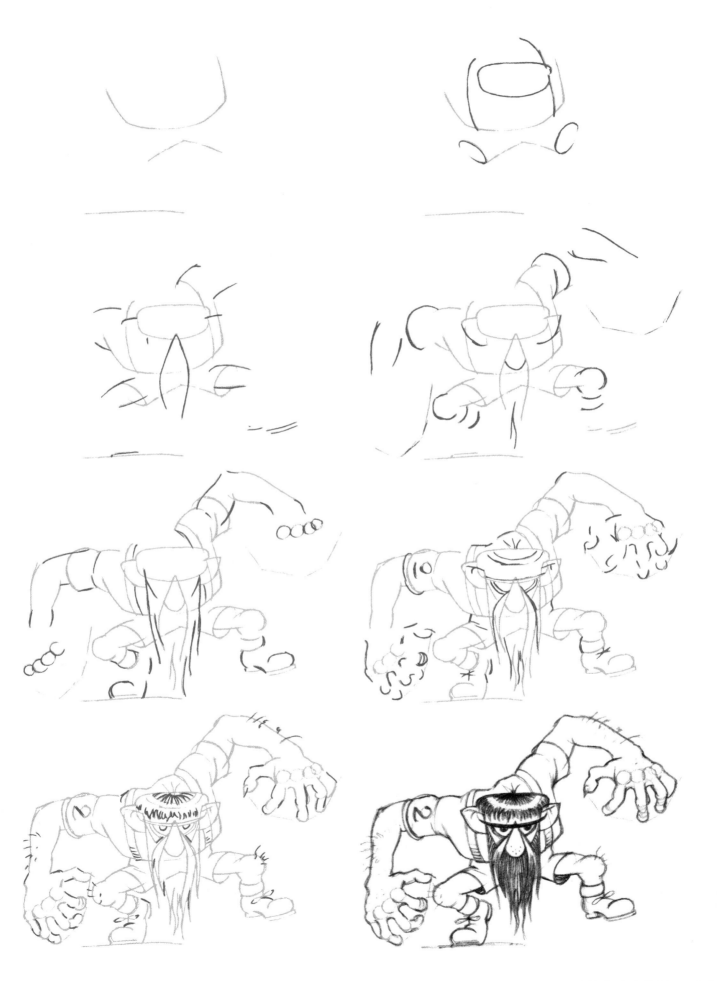

GNOME BURT 000

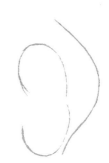
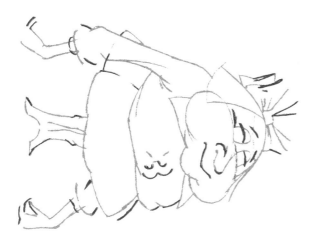
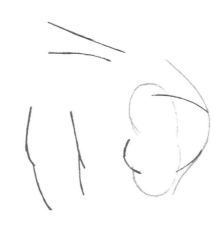
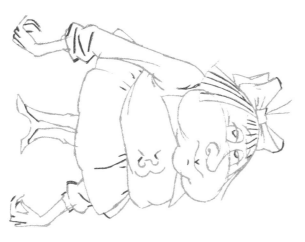
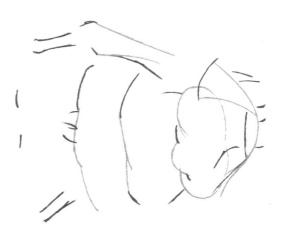
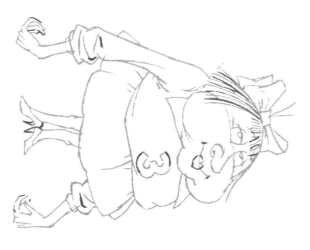
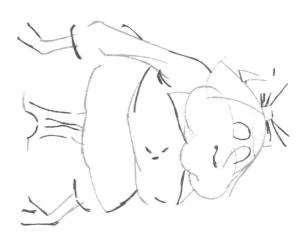
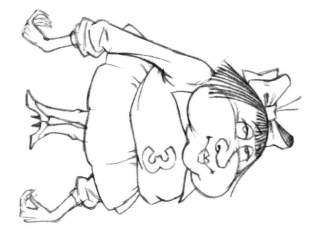

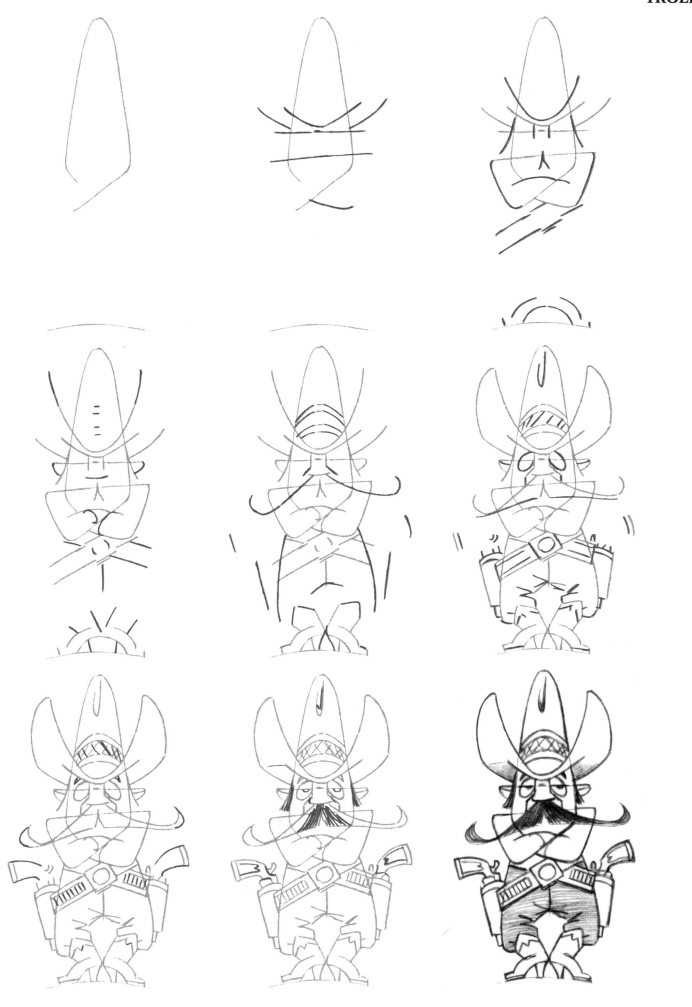

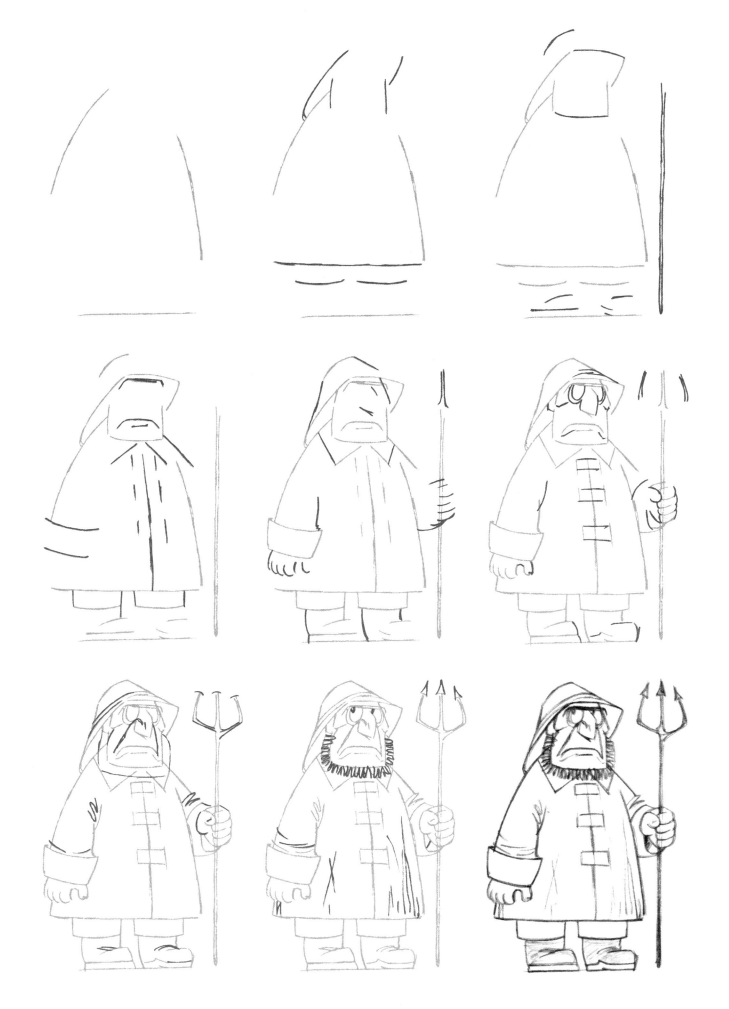

HARB ORPA TROLL

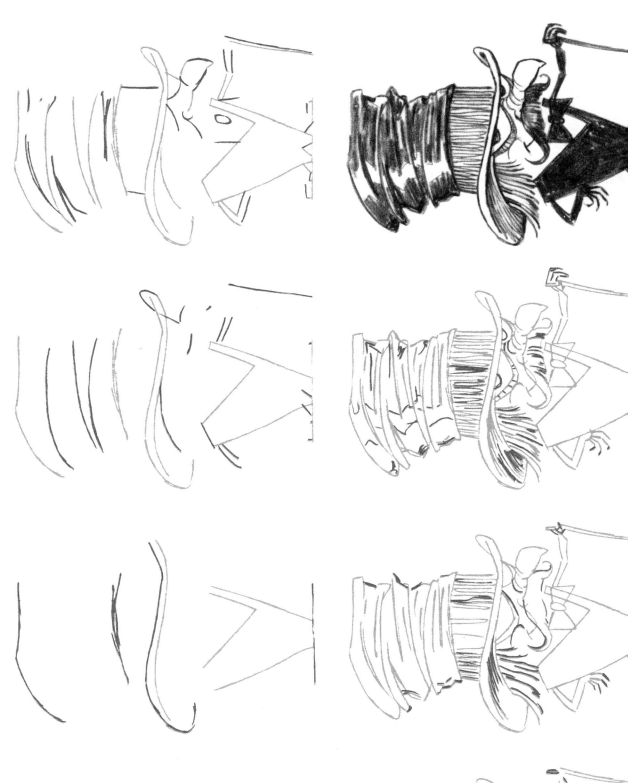

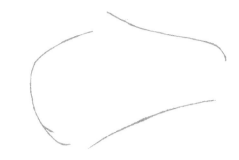

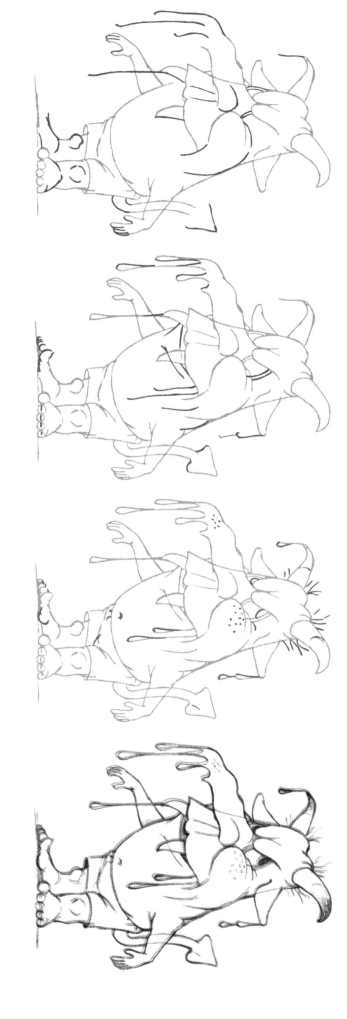

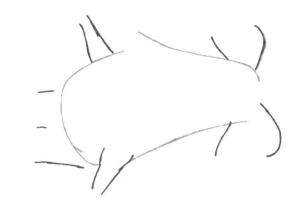

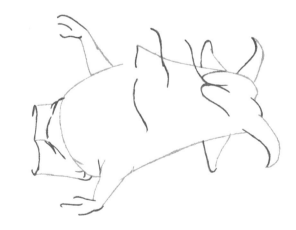

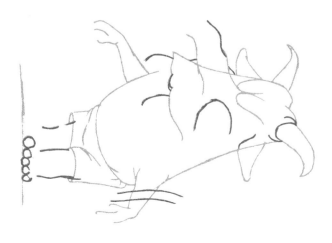

DEMON SSDRIBBLE

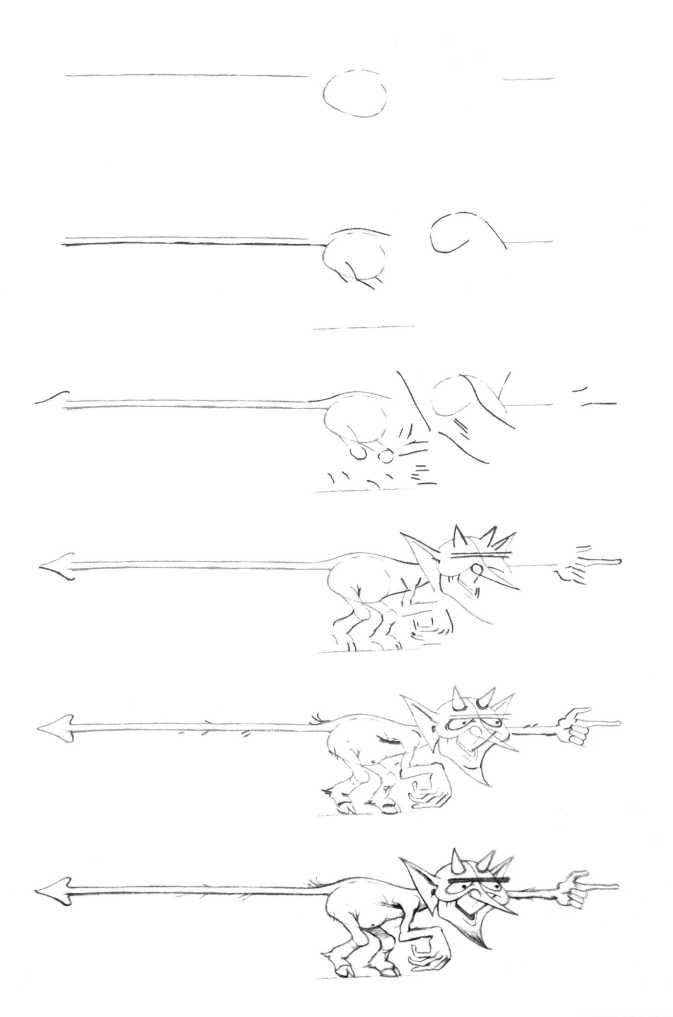

DEMON STRAIGHT

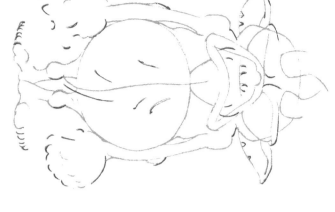
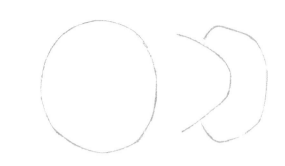

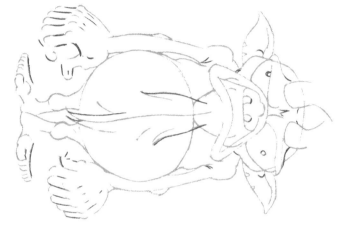
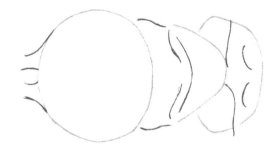

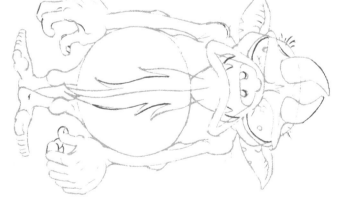
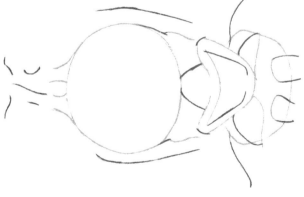

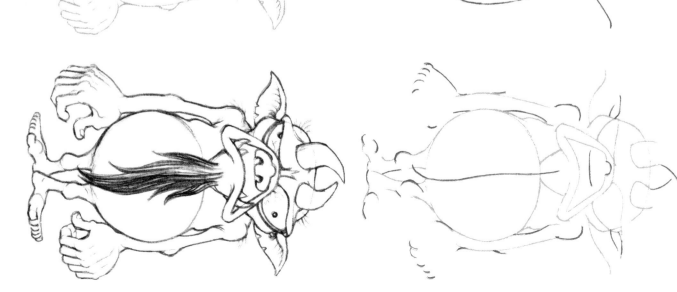

DEMON EYE IKKILL

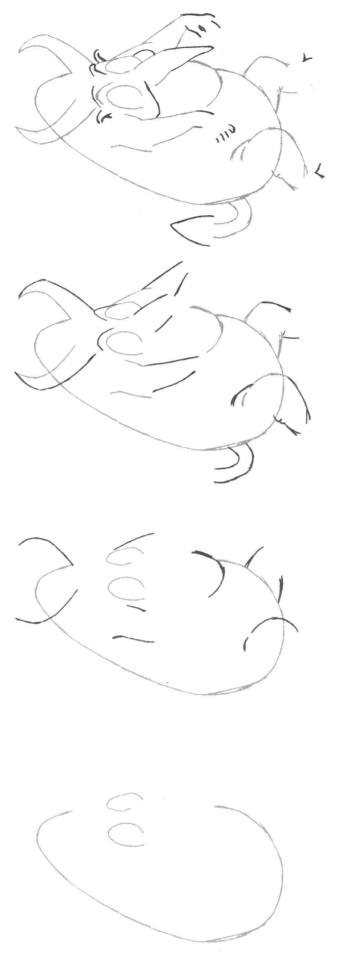
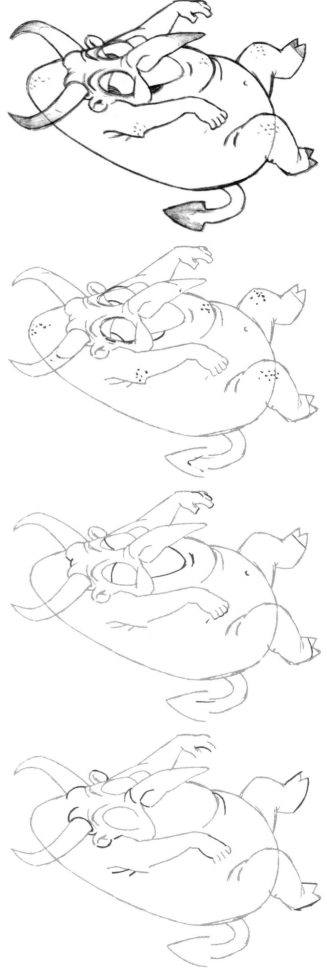

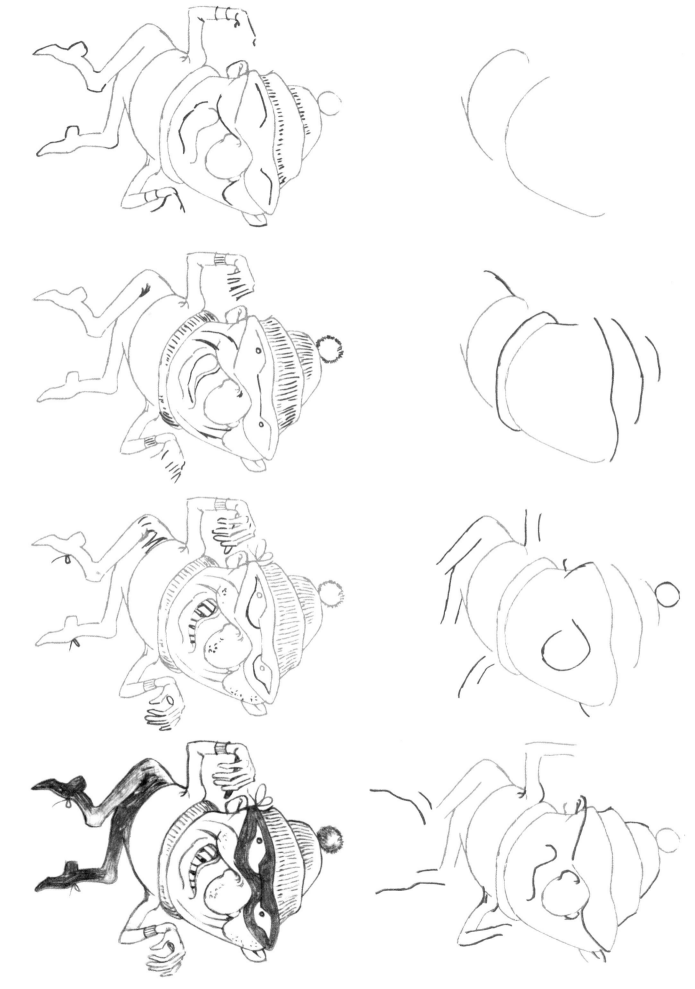

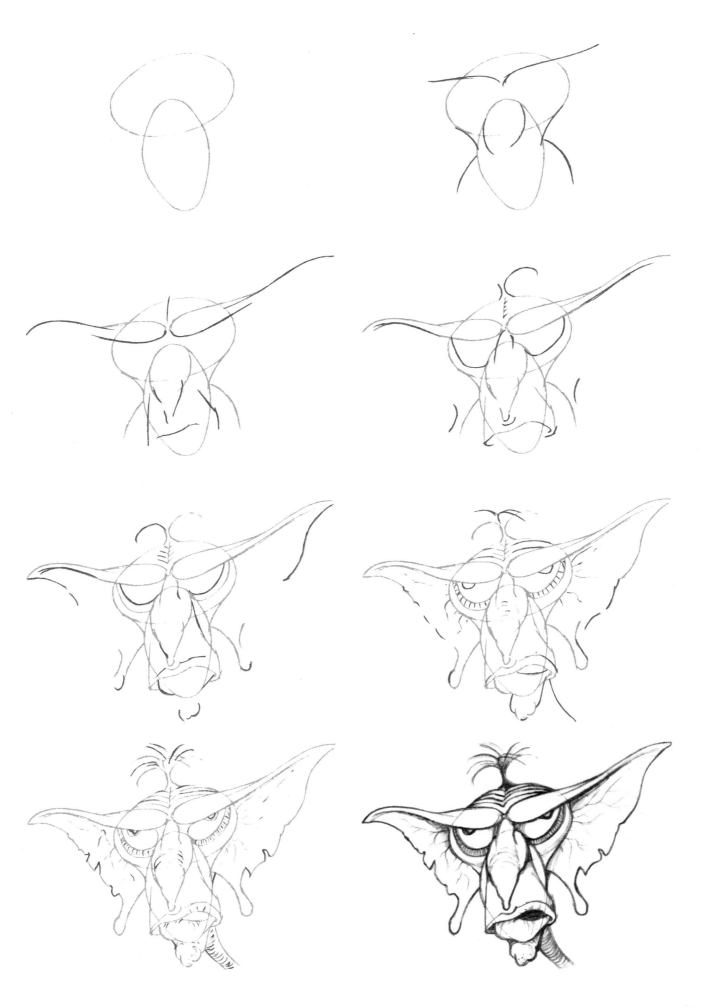

IMP EARIE AL

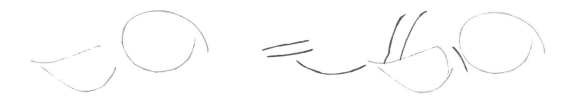
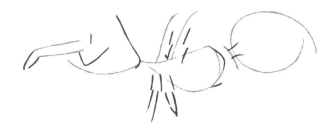
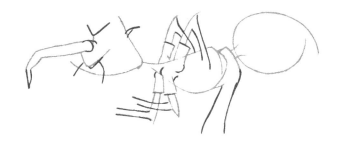
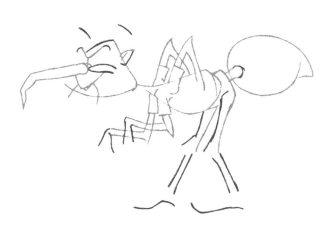
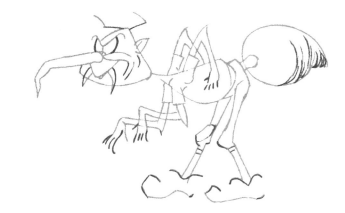
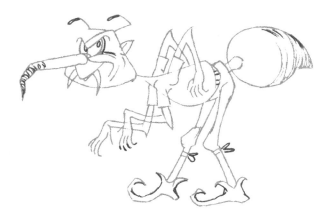
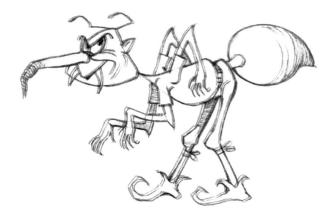

IMP ORT ANT

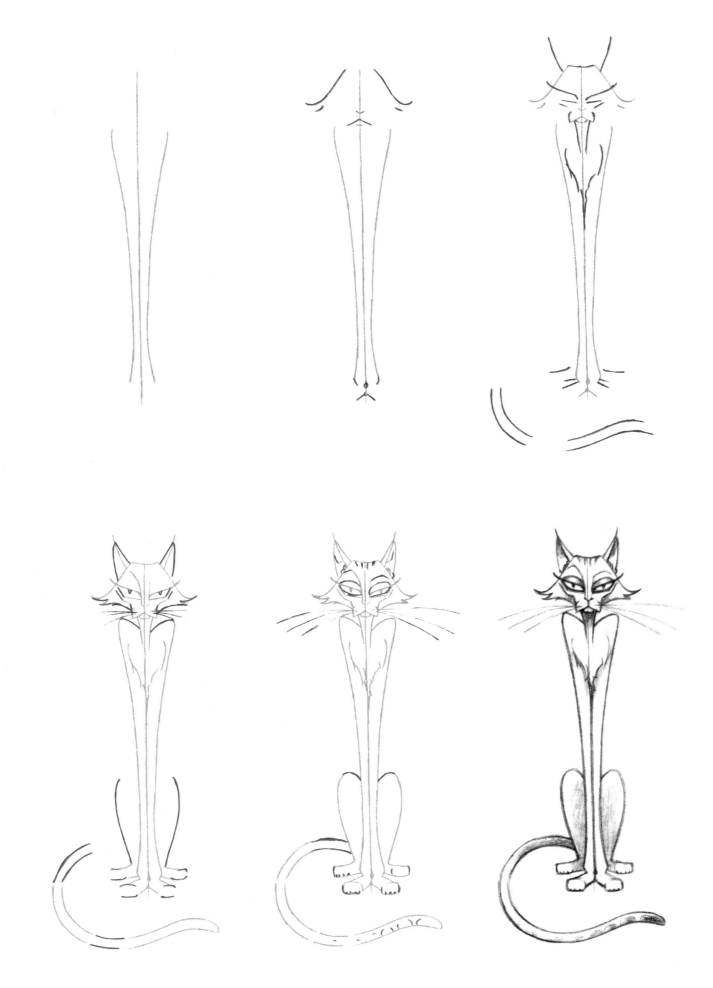

SOPHIE STICK CAT

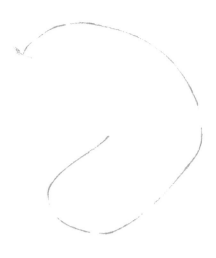
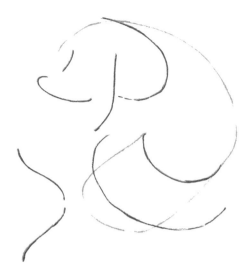
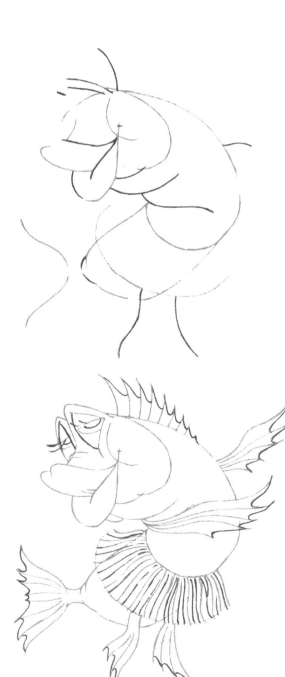
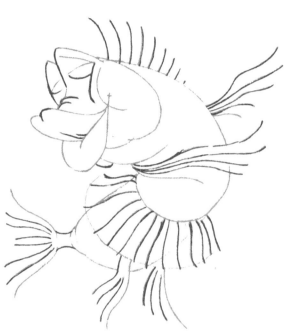
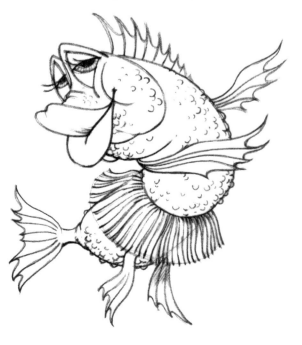

TRA PICKLEFISH

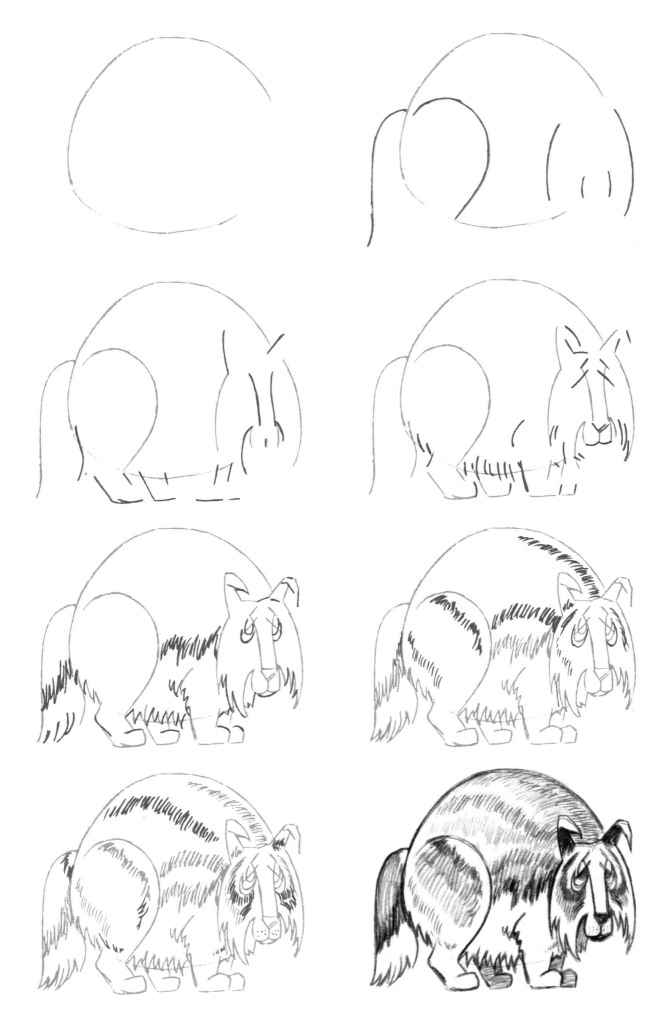

MELON COLLIE

DINA SOURS

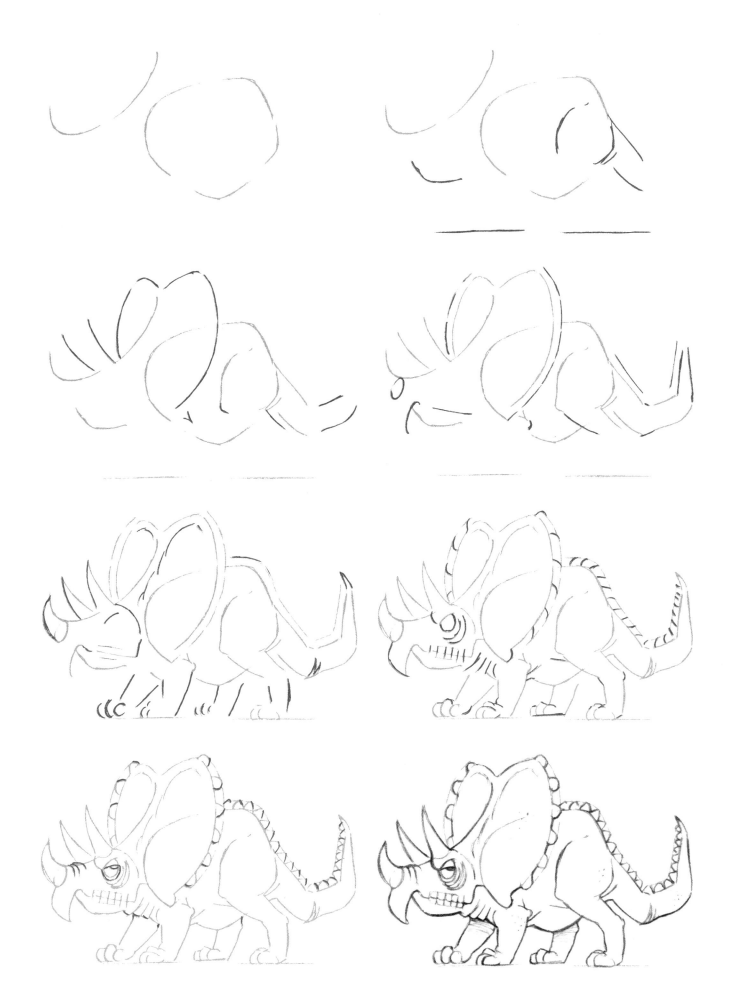

SARA TRITOPS

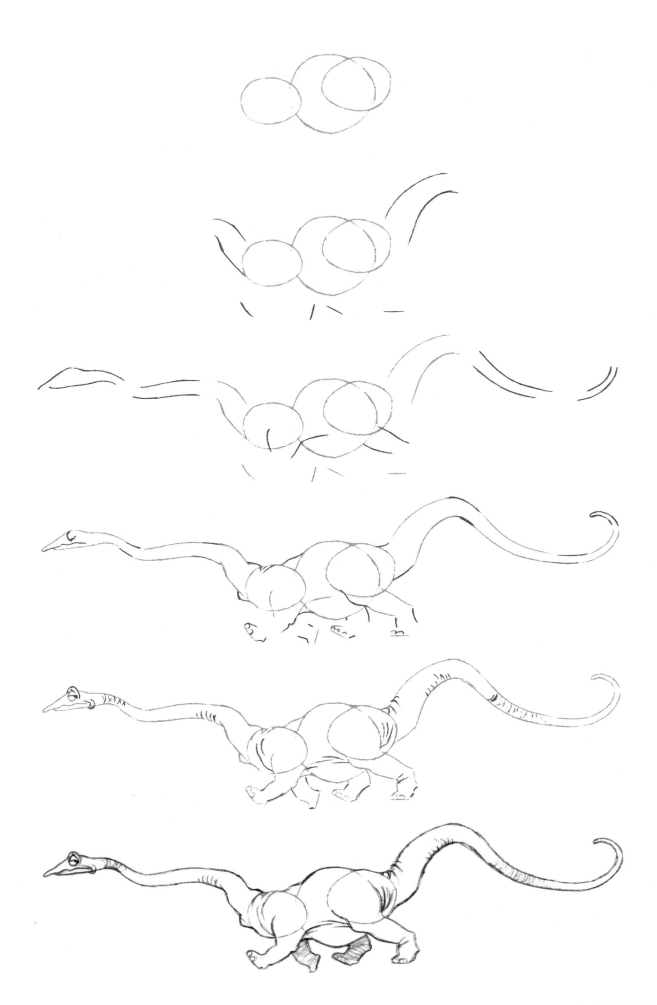

DIPPY LODDACUSS

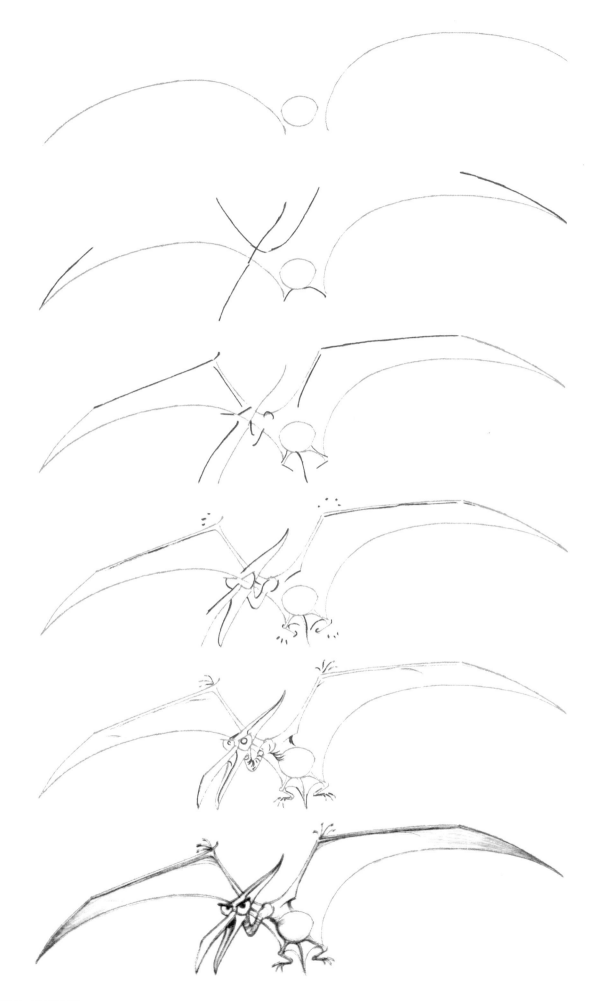

TERRY ANNA DUNN

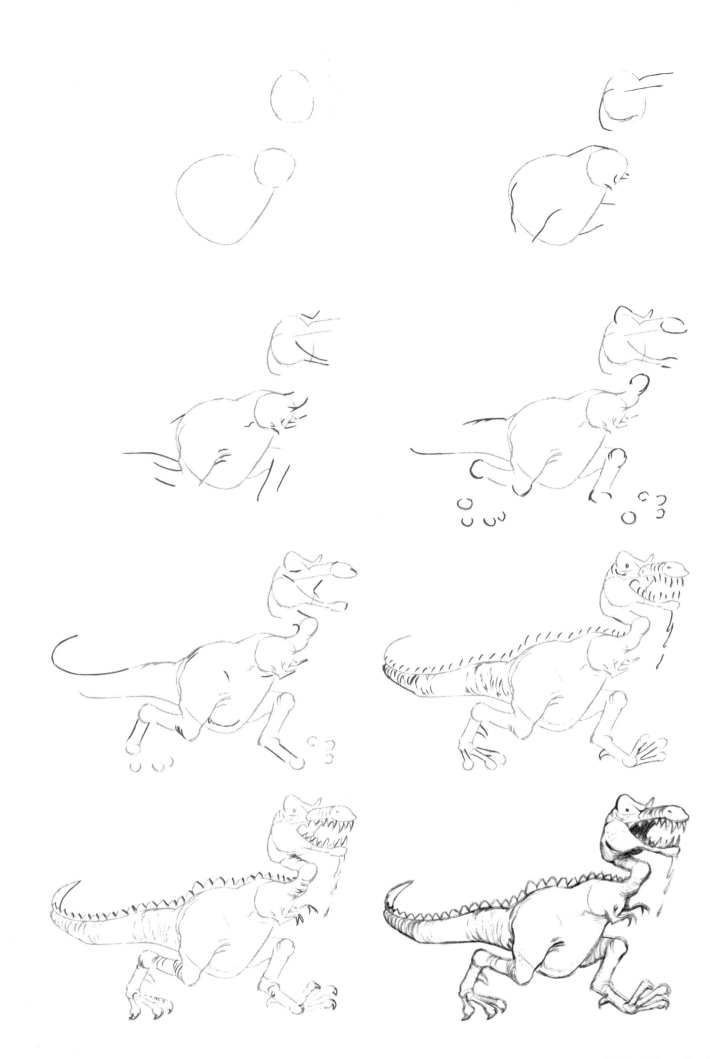

TYRONE IZ SORUS

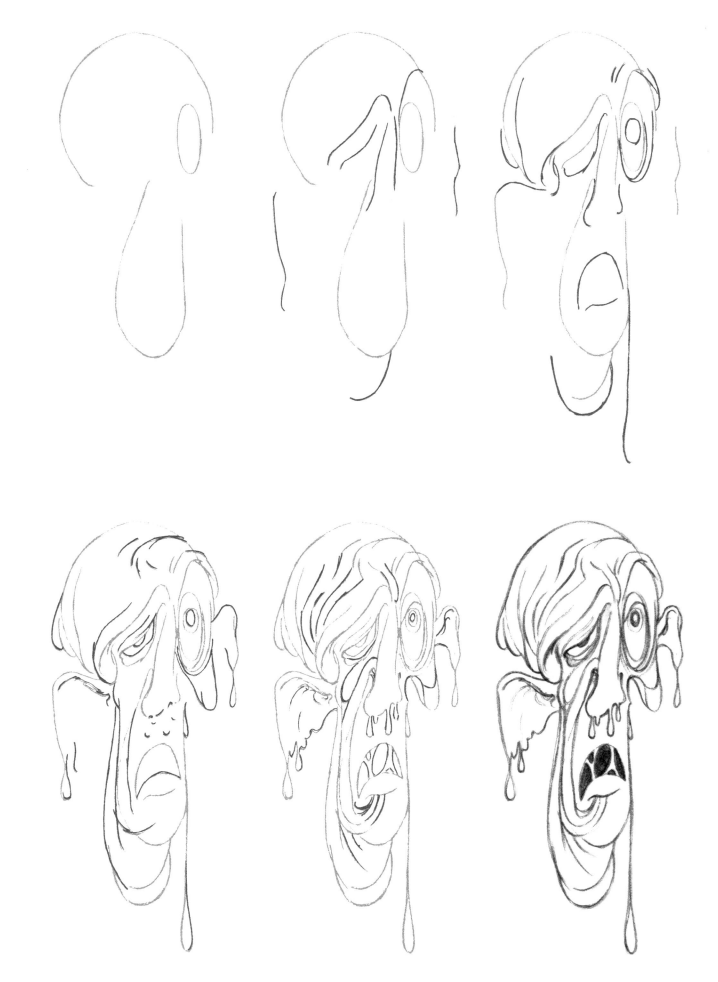

DRIBBLE PUSS

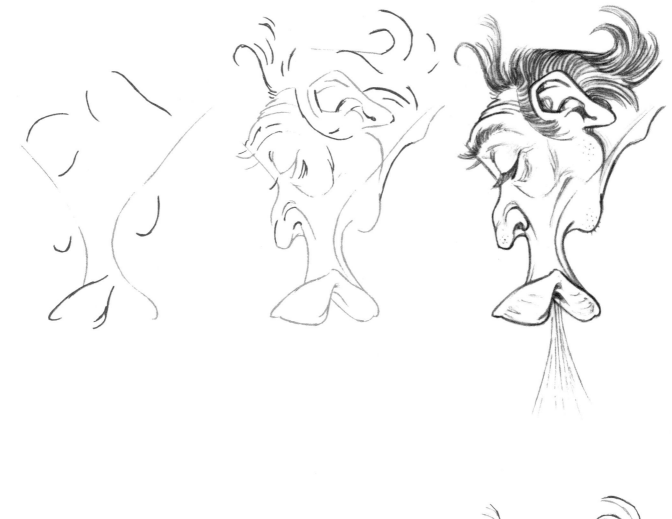

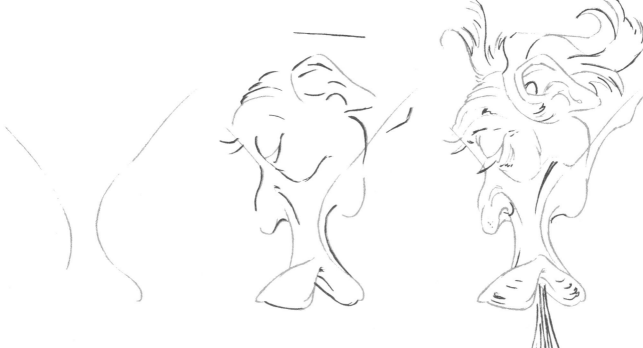

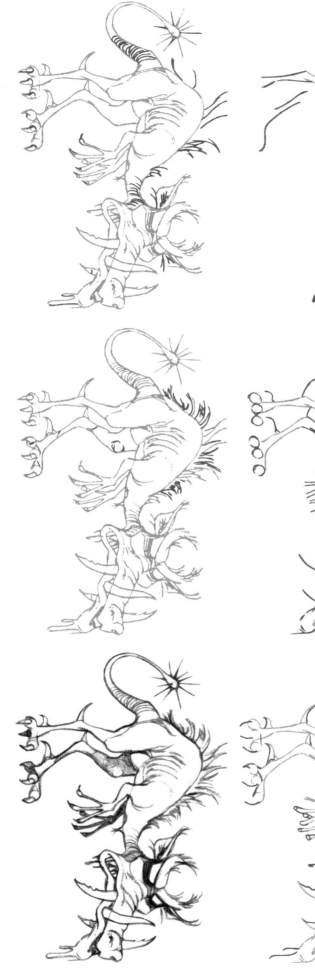
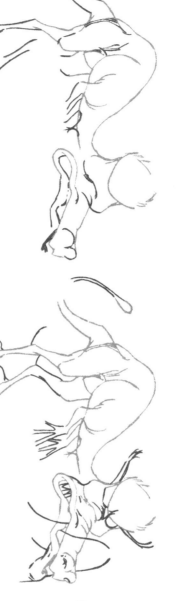
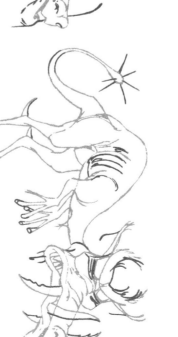
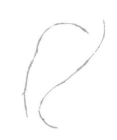
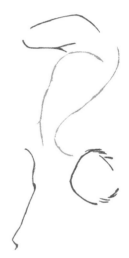
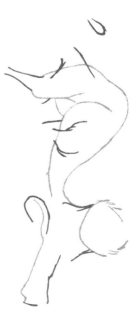

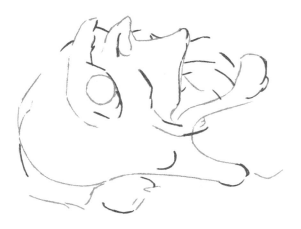
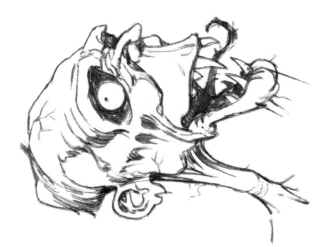
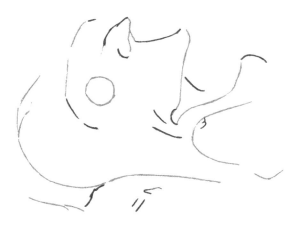
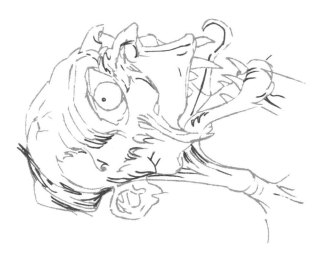
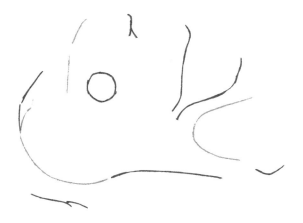
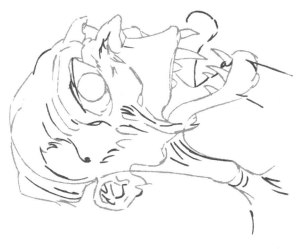
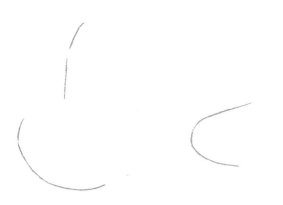
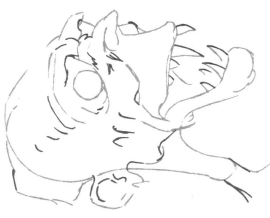

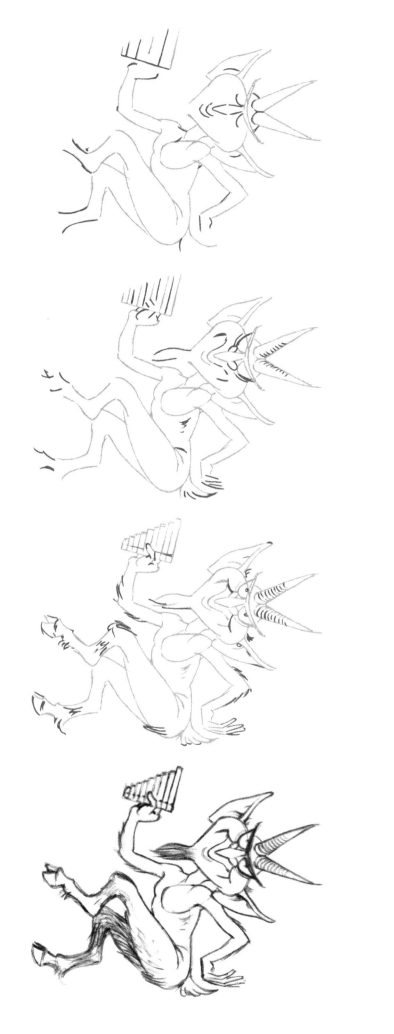
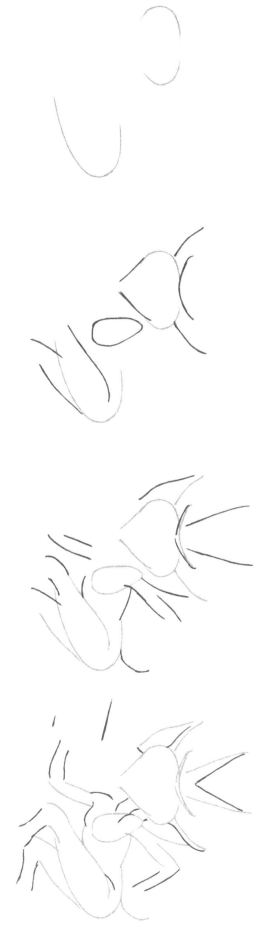

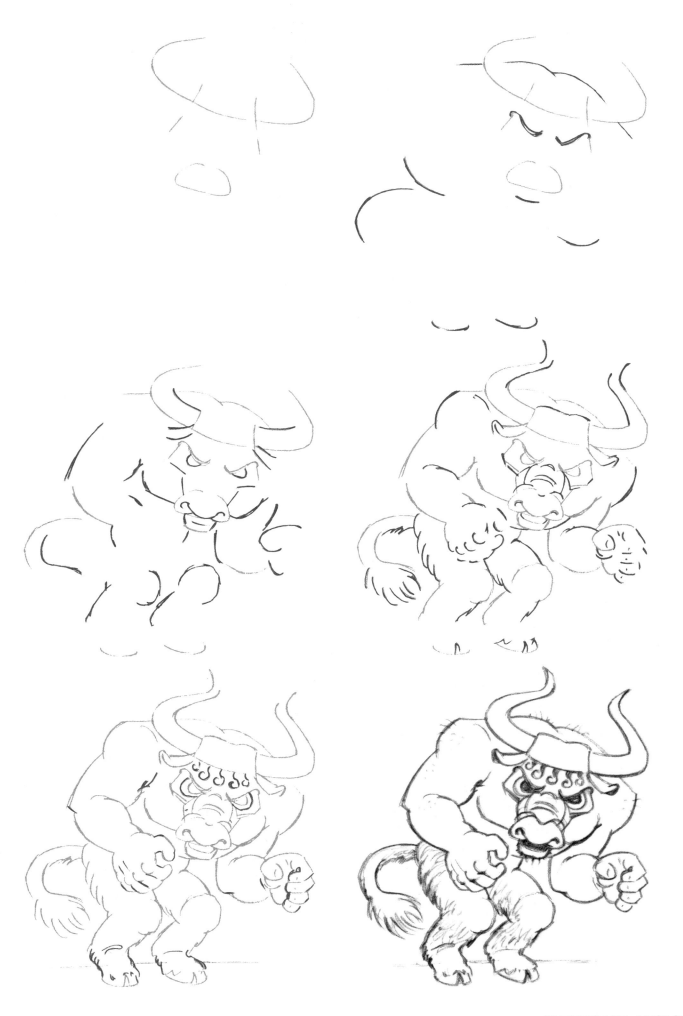

AWESOME MINOTAUR

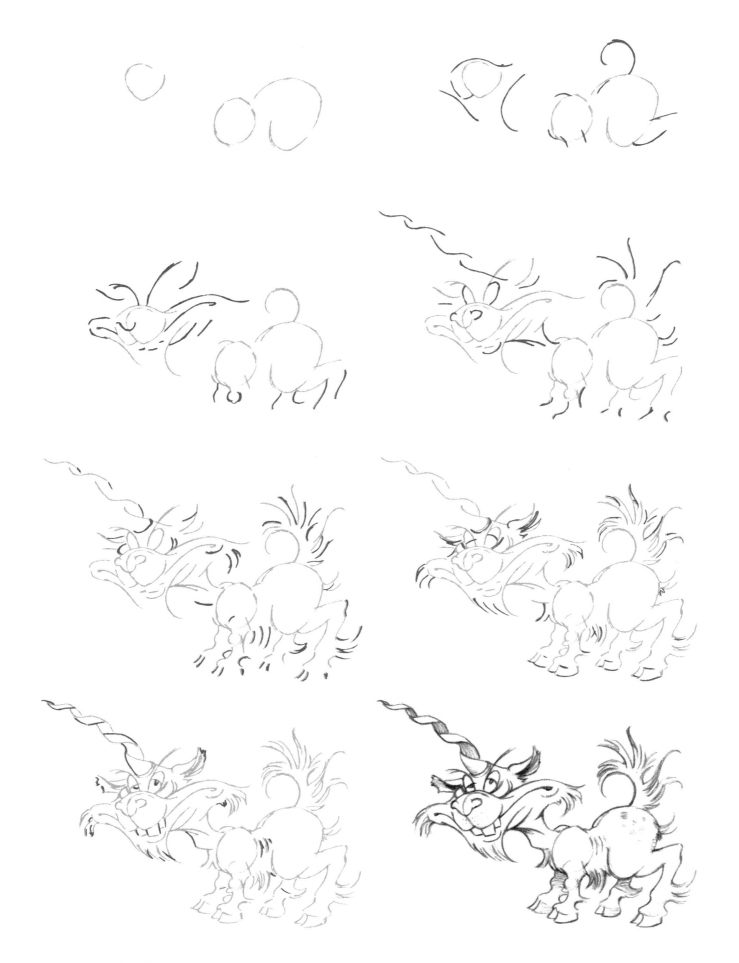

LOONY PUNYCORN

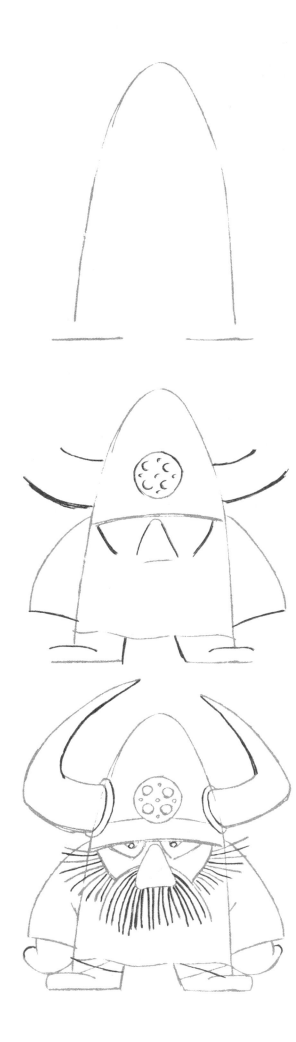
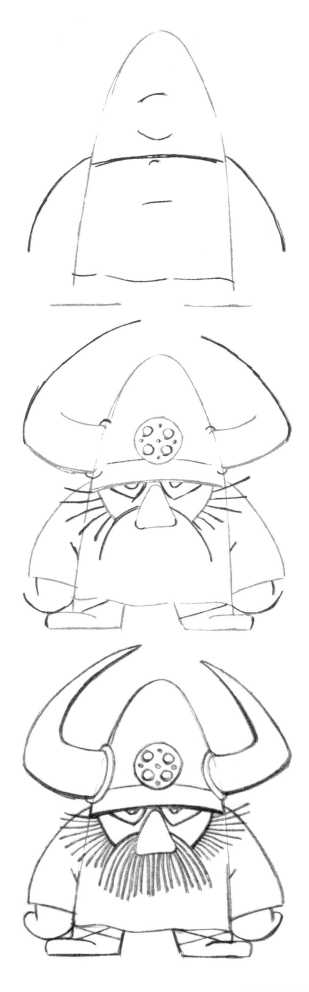

MIKE THE VIKE

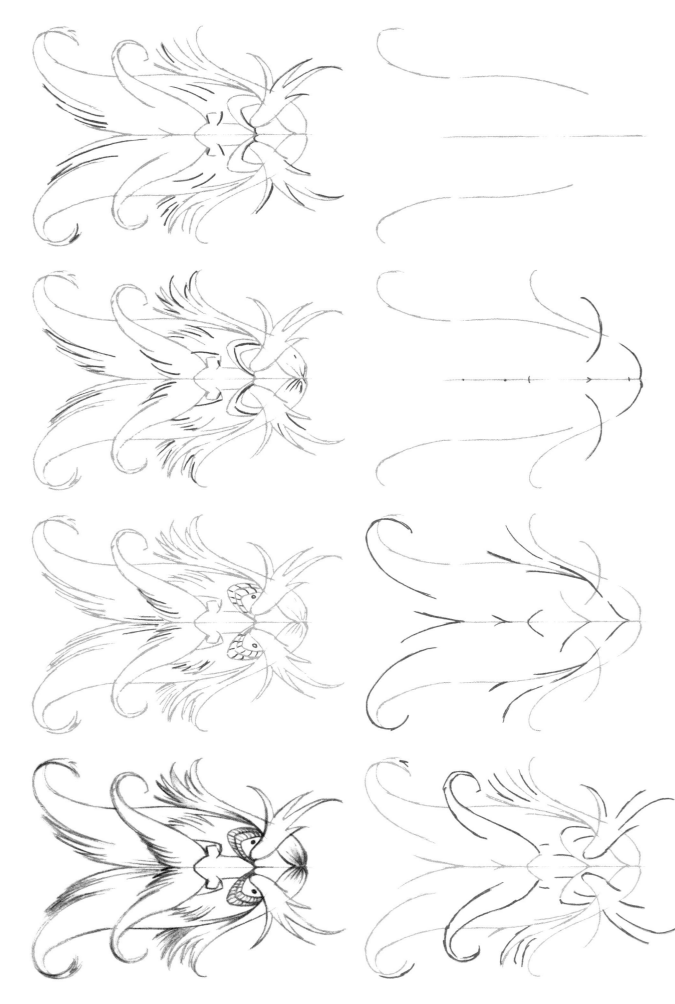

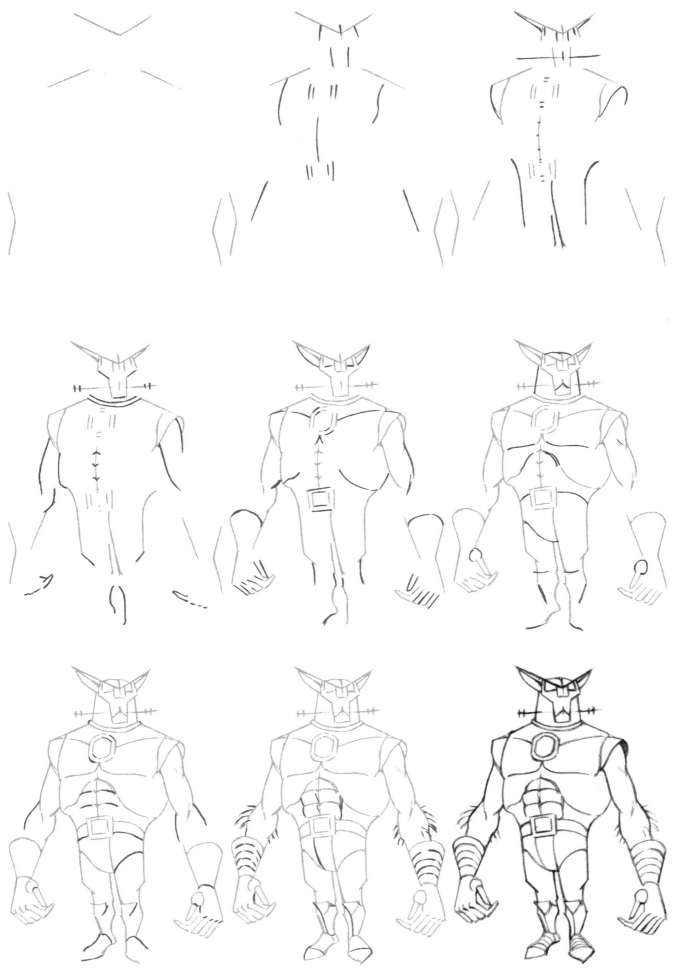

DIZZ TRAWYER

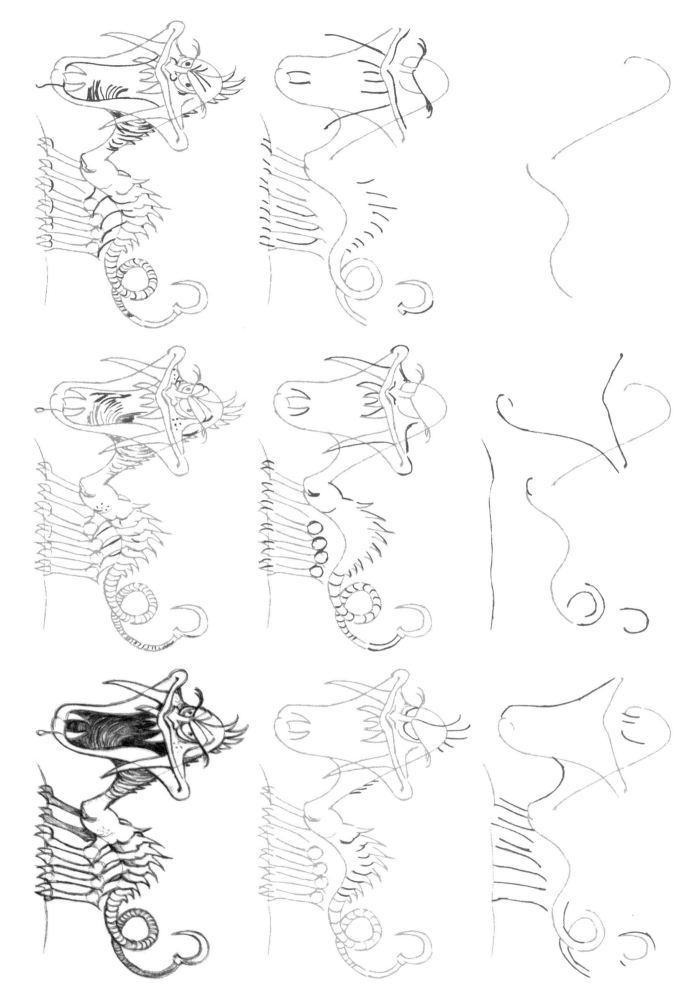

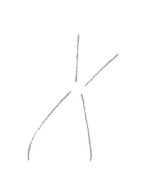
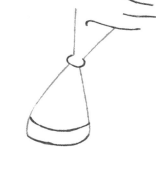

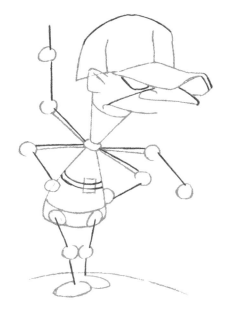
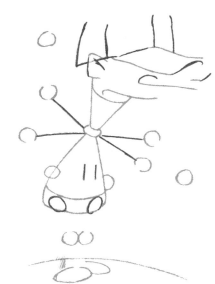
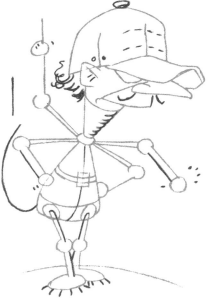
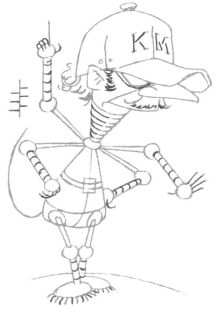
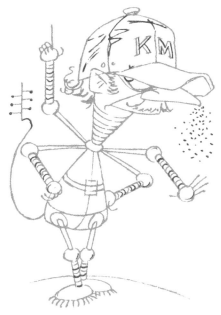
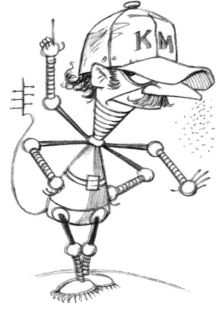

KHAZ MCDUST

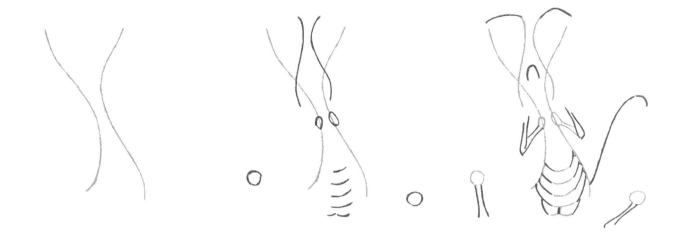

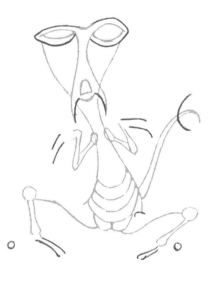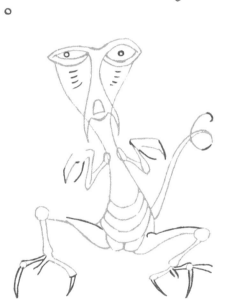

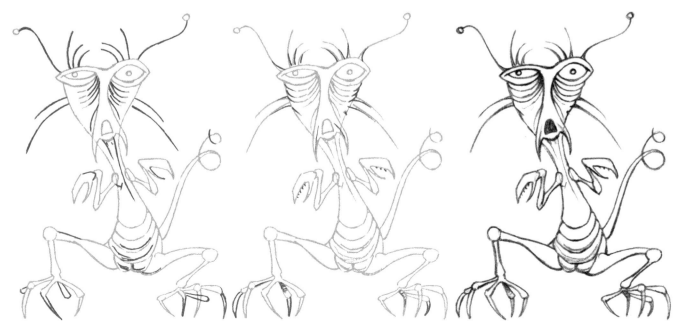

MINI MOOM

LEE J. AMES joined the Doubleday list in 1962, and since that time his popular drawing books have sold close to one and a half million copies. Utilizing a unique, step-by-step method to guide the young artist's hand, Ames's "Draw 50" books have inspired the creativity of countless children (and adults).

His artistic experience runs the gamut from working at Walt Disney Studios in the days when *Fantasia* and *Pinocchio* were created to teaching at New York City's School of Visual Arts to running his own advertising agency. In addition, he has illustrated over 150 books, from preschool picture books to postgraduate texts.

When not working in his studio, Lee can be found on the tennis courts in Long Island, New York, where he currently lives with his wife, Jocelyn.

DRAW 50 FOR HOURS OF FUN!

Using Lee J. Ames's proven, step-by-step method of drawing instruction, you can easily learn to draw animals, monsters, airplanes, cars, sharks, buildings, dinosaurs, famous cartoons, and so much more! Millions of people have learned to draw by using the award-winning "Draw 50" technique. Now you can too!

COLLECT THE ENTIRE DRAW 50 SERIES!

The Draw 50 Series books are available from your local bookstore. You may also order direct (make a copy of this form to order). Titles are paperback, unless otherwise indicated.

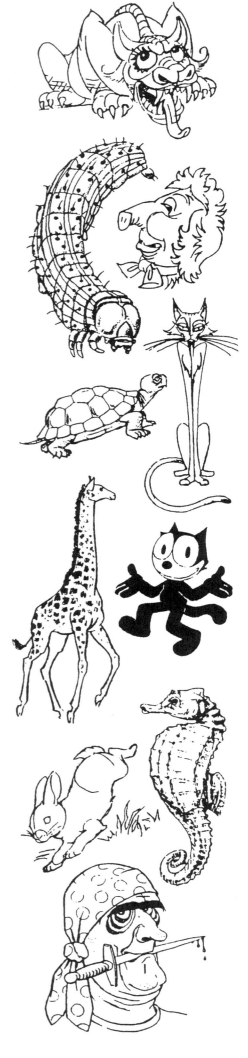

ISBN	TITLE	PRICE	QTY	TOTAL
23629-8	Airplanes, Aircraft, and Spacecraft	$8.95/$11.95 Can	× _____ =	_____
49145-X	Aliens	$8.95/$11.95 Can	× _____ =	_____
19519-2	Animals	$8.95/$11.95 Can	× _____ =	_____
24638-2	Athletes	$8.95/$11.95 Can	× _____ =	_____
26767-3	Beasties and Yugglies and Turnover Uglies and Things That Go Bump in the Night	$8.95/$11.95 Can	× _____ =	_____
47163-7	Birds	$8.95/$11.95 Can	× _____ =	_____
47006-1	Birds (hardcover)	$13.95/$18.95 Can	× _____ =	_____
23630-1	Boats, Ships, Trucks, and Trains	$8.95/$11.95 Can	× _____ =	_____
41777-2	Buildings and Other Structures	$8.95/$11.95 Can	× _____ =	_____
24639-0	Cars, Trucks, and Motorcycles	$8.95/$11.95 Can	× _____ =	_____
24640-4	Cats	$8.95/$11.95 Can	× _____ =	_____
42449-3	Creepy Crawlies	$8.95/$11.95 Can	× _____ =	_____
19520-6	Dinosaurs and Other Prehistoric Animals	$8.95/$11.95 Can	× _____ =	_____
23431-7	Dogs	$8.95/$11.95 Can	× _____ =	_____
46985-3	Endangered Animals	$8.95/$11.95 Can	× _____ =	_____
19521-4	Famous Cartoons	$8.95/$11.95 Can	× _____ =	_____
23432-5	Famous Faces	$8.95/$11.95 Can	× _____ =	_____
47150-5	Flowers, Trees, and Other Plants	$8.95/$11.95 Can	× _____ =	_____
26770-3	Holiday Decorations	$8.95/$11.95 Can	× _____ =	_____
17642-2	Horses	$8.95/$11.95 Can	× _____ =	_____
17639-2	Monsters	$8.95/$11.95 Can	× _____ =	_____
41194-4	People	$8.95/$11.95 Can	× _____ =	_____
47162-9	People of the Bible	$8.95/$11.95 Can	× _____ =	_____
47005-3	People of the Bible (hardcover)	$13.95/$19.95 Can	× _____ =	_____
26768-1	Sharks, Whales, and Other Sea Creatures	$8.95/$11.95 Can	× _____ =	_____
14154-8	Vehicles	$8.95/$11.95 Can	× _____ =	_____
	Shipping and handling	**(add $2.50 per order)** ×	_____ =	_____
		TOTAL		_____

Please send me the title(s) I have indicated above. I am enclosing $_____.

Send check or money order in U.S. funds only (no C.O.D.s or cash, please). Make check payable to Random House, Inc. Allow 4–6 weeks for delivery. Prices and availability subject to change without notice.

Name: _____

Address: _____ Apt. #_____

City: _____ State: _____ Zip: _____

Send completed coupon and payment to:

Random House, Inc.
Customer Service
400 Hahn Rd.
Westminster, MD 21157

BROADWAY